D0825105

# FAMILY REUNION

BOOKS BY JOSEPH BABINSKY (SELF-PUBLISHED)

*Faces of Joseph – Journal of Self-Discovery (Memoir) 2004*
*The Magical Dream Forest (Stories for Children) 2008*
*Gentle River Flow (Essays, Stories and Poems) 2005*
*The Babinsky Family (Genealogy and Narrative) 2008*
*Matthew's Choice (A Novel, inspired by A Course in Miracles)*
*I Thought I Killed Jesus (An Historic Novel) 2006*
*Divine Love Flowing (Introduction to the Padgett Messages)*
*The Human Soul (A study, based on the Padgett Messages)*
*The Choice (A brief memoir) 2010*
*Climb the Mountain – Paths Taken (Memoir) 2016*

COMPILATION OF WRITINGS OF JAMES PADGETT

*Book of Truths*
*Little Book of Truths*
*Teachings of Jesus*
*Divine Love – Transforming the Soul, Five Volume Edition*
*Messages from Heaven*
*The Way of Divine Love*
*Divine Love – Greatest of all Truths*
*Facts Revealed from the Spirit World*
*Realms of the Spirit World*
*Preachers Speak from Heaven*

OUT-OF-PRINT BOOKS REPLUBLISHED

*Christ in Tibet – M. MacDonald-Bayne*
*Life in the World Unseen – Anthony Borgia*
*Through the Mists – R. J. Lees*
*Elysian – R. J. Lees*
*Gate of Heaven – R. J. Lees*

ALL THE ABOVE BOOKS ARE SELF-PUBLISHED, AVAILABLE AT:

www.lulu.com/spotlight/josephbabinsky

ABOUT THE FRONT COVER

The photograph on the front cover is by Sandy Coffin of New York, NY, used with her permission. It is Lake George, Silver Bay, eastern New York State, the location of several Babinsky family reunions.

*To Richard —*

# FAMILY REUNION
### Afterlife Contact

*AREI and "Afterlife Contact"*
*This book could be interesting !*

*Thank you for your friendship —*

*Joseph*
*Jan. 24, 2019*

FAMILY REUNION
Afterlife Contact

By Joseph Babinsky

Copyright © 2018 Joseph Babinsky

All rights reserved under International and Pan American Copyright Conventions. No part of this book may be stored, reproduced or transmitted in any form, or by any means without the expressed written permission of the author.

FIRST EDITION August 2015
REVISED EDITION May 2018

ISBN 978-1-329-15378-3

This book is made available by

GRP – *Gentle River Publishing*
Prescott, Arizona
U.S.A.

A self-published book through:
Lulu Enterprises, Inc.
3101 Hillsborough Street
Raleigh, NC 27607
Websites: www.lulu.com
            www.lulu.com/spotlight/josephbabinsky

*"Progress is the one law of the universe that exists always, and man, when he gets in condition, will always be the object and subject of that law."*

Jesus

(James Padgett: June 7, 1920)

*"The basic subject of my writings is about the greatest thing in the whole universe. The subject is God and His great love. How great is that? What a story! And I haven't really begun to tell the story the way it really is. That's why I write and continue to write."*

Suggestion for Joseph from Celestial Angels
*Family Reunion*, page 159.

# CONTENTS

# FOREWORD
By Joseph Babinsky

The beginning of my life was far from a condition to provide stability and happiness for a child. How do you teach a two-year-old to stop calling her mommy? In 1937 they had to do this to me and six other siblings. It was the Great Depression. Our family was poor and we moved to an orphanage. Mom and Dad were hired to work there under the condition their children were not permitted to be recognized as family. We lived as orphans four years, and when we departed in 1941, I had to learn how to live in a family. I remember my older brother, Charles, pointing to a stranger, saying, "See that man? He is our dad. Call him daddy or father. Do not say, *Mr. Teacher*." Charles used the Hungarian language when he said 'Mr. Teacher'. He did the same when he talked about mother.

Three years after reuniting as a family unit, tragedy visited our family. Charles was ten years older than me and my favorite brother. He died in 1944 as the result of injuries suffered during World War II in France. We never saw him again. They shipped Charles home sealed shut in a casket. There was a funeral and following it, the family gathered in the living room of our home. My dad asked each one what we planned to do when the war was over. Because I was the youngest child, he asked me last: "What do you want to do when you grow up?" I mumbled but had no clear answer. I was a nine and never understood any of this. I did not believe Charles was dead. I looked for him every day until eventually

I gave up.

My life after this followed a winding trail. In 1953, after high school, I started engineering school at the University of Buffalo, and completed two years. I was drafted into the U.S. Army and after two years of rugged experiences, yet, somehow, also successful, I returned home and resumed engineering studies. I found myself unhappy and restless, so I quit the university and transferred to a small liberal arts college located in Illinois, where I changed my major to Philosophy. This change was good for me. I began to give creative thought about what I wanted to do with my life. I completed this work with a degree, and continued my studies in graduate school, and received a Master's Degree in Theology. Following the footsteps of my father and an older brother, I chose to become a minister and was ordained in the Presbyterian Church.

Though I was successful in Christian ministry, restlessness remained, which eventually led me to explore other directions. In the beginning of this change, I had no plans to leave the Church permanently. But, over the years I slowly broke away from organized Christianity. When I did this, I discovered a new world waiting for me. This new path led me to a twenty-year search for answers. Surprisingly, on this self-directed vision quest, I developed a deeper love for our *Creator*. I found an inner happiness not based on dogma, Church doctrines, or an authority outside of who I am inside. It required seventy years for me to finally realize happiness is a deep inner place of peace based solely on knowing who and what I am. My journey continued, yet not as it had been.

Something amazing happened on my seventieth birthday. Words written with my own hand startled me. I was dumbstruck to see them on the paper. I celebrated my birthday by going for a walk at a lake located six miles from our home. When I was younger I hiked, but in my later years I changed from hiking to slow walking. The difference is that I pause often to look at views of beauty I see in the surroundings, take photos, or simply stop often to watch birds who love this same location. The main trail at the lake follows the shoreline through magnificent pine trees that form part of our National

Forest. I tire easily, so stopped to rest near a thick tree. I leaned back and wrote in my journal. After several pages of reflective writing, I finished with five words: *I am a happy man.* Never before had I declared unequivocally such a positive statement about my life. This was a new thing. It was not the way of my life. Conscious awareness of happiness eluded me.

One short year later, a few weeks from my seventy-first birthday, I was not unhappy, not restless, not searching for a new experience, and, yet, I had an unexpected surprise that prompted me to make the most important choice of my already long life. Looking back, I feel I was given an opportunity to see higher paths—higher realms than I had ever imagined existed. I was given opportunity to listen to angel voices. No, I did not die and visit heaven. It happened that I was writing a novel, and in order to find additional background details, with innocence I searched places on the Internet that eventually led me to a website where I found more than I was seeking.

I read about a man one-hundred years ago who received communications from high realms of the afterlife. James Padgett is the man referenced. He was born in Washington, D.C., where he became an attorney. After a number of years, Helen, his wife, became ill, and died. Though a religious man in the Methodist Church, he was distraught, and sought help from a psychic. The psychic gave James a word from his wife and something more. James was informed he had the ability to communicate directly with Helen. He was encouraged to go home and practice automatic writing. He did, and the experiment worked. At the age of sixty-two, James began receiving communications from Helen regularly. This happened in 1914. One day, James learned that Jesus of the Bible desired to write. Because he still harbored religious beliefs that influenced him, he refused the initial invitation. Slowly, he relented, and began recording messages from Jesus until 1923, the year that he died.

The story of James Padgett inspired me to study his writings. This was no small task. His writings totaled over one thousand messages. Through years of study, I learned a new appreciation of our Creator and the Great Love He has for all

His children, including me. I learned that I my true identity is that I am a soul, and that the human soul can actually be transformed into a Divine Soul through the Great Love freely given to every person who desires such change—and asks. I have been doing this experiment twelve years, and discovered I am slowly being changed. As a result, the happiness experienced when I was seventy, has slowly deepened and grown richer. I did not return to religion. I turned to an experiential relationship with our Creator—Who we call Heavenly Father. And my identity is new: *I am a soul, clothed in a spirit-body, and temporarily inhabiting a physical body.*

The next step in my vision quest led me back to my birth-family: Nine members in my family had already died, and I developed a curiosity whether I might receive personal communications from my family now living in the afterlife, in a way similar to the experience of James Padgett. I had no motive or desire to become a popular medium. Thus, I began slowly as an extremely cautious person. When I started, I was surprised who came first from my family to write. It was not someone I had fond memories of. It was my own biological father.

I was puzzled that my dad would be the first from my family to come to write. I was a sixteen-year-old boy when he died and, truthfully, I disliked him intensely. In later years I went through much pain to accept my feelings and be healed of them. I was a grown man, and no longer harbored anger toward him. But still, I asked, what purpose did his presence have? The next day my father returned, and I invited him to write. I welcomed his return, and we became friends. Plus, he is a great help to me while learning the craft of writing messages from the afterlife.

Next to come and write was my mother. She no longer had the voice I remember. She spoke clearly and distinctly, and with a new kindness and love.

After mother, came the sister I never met. She died one day after birth, in July of 1924. I did not write with a little girl, but a mature woman. Her name is Ana. She is a spiritual leader of the family. She was raised by highly evolved spirits, who introduced her to the teachings of Jesus, the same teachings I was introduced to on earth through James Padgett. Ana is the one who introduced God's Great Love to each of my family that passed from life on earth to the new life in the spirit-world. Ana was present to welcome Charles when he died at the age of nineteen during World War II. In messages I received from Ana and Charles, I learned about Charles' transition to his new life in the spirit-world. It was a memorable day when I received my first communication from Charles. It was a wonderful reunion, a letter I will always cherish.

I am now an eighty-three-year-old man and experiencing a happier state than I was when I scribed notes in my journal while resting against a tree in the forest on my seventy-first birthday. The greater happiness did not happen in an instant. In early 2006, when I was introduced to the writings of James Padgett that I found on Geoff Cutler's website and began to read the messages James received from Jesus, my transformation began slowly. Change and the potential of progress remain while I am on earth. When I pass, the journey will continue in the afterlife on paths only now dimly seen.

I offer this new and improved edition of the book, *Family Reunion*. I pray and hope you will find it not only interesting, but life-changing.

Joseph Babinsky
Prescott, Arizona
May 29, 2018

# INTRODUCTION
By Geoff Cutler

When I heard that my dear friend Joseph had a new book out, I was overjoyed. I have so much enjoyed his previous writings.

Then I heard that this book, *Family Reunion*, contained spirit communications that Joseph had received, and not only was I excited, but also very curious. You see, even though Joseph is a very adept writer, and clearly both sensitive and open to spirit leadings, I was unaware that he had the ability to hear spirit clearly enough to take dictation. So, I pounced on the book the moment it arrived from the printer. I was not disappointed.

I first met Joseph via the marvels of the Internet, in April of 2006, a few days after he discovered my website. I have a rather eclectic website which contains a very great number of spirit communications and references to a large number of books which include spirit communications.

So it came about that Joseph wanted to discuss a book he was much enamoured of: "A Course in Miracles." He asked me to compare it to what we call "The Padgett Messages." This I was able to do because I also appreciated ACIM, even as I prefer the Padgett material, and I managed to whet his appetite to study the latter. That was the trigger for us to become firm friends and the beginning of a new journey of discovery for Joseph.

I finally met Joseph in person in 2014, when he travelled to Australia.

Over the years that I have known him, he has shared a bit about his life and of course the very large family he was the youngest member of. To finally hear from many of these now in spirit is a real treasure. And to hear exactly how they found the very same spiritual path that Joseph now follows is even more intriguing.

Joseph's own path has been a long, steady, determined effort to reach more and yet more truth. He has in fact dedicated his entire life to this spiritual search. I do not want to spoil the story by revealing the amazing discovery he has made: I leave that to the reader. Suffice it to say that I found this book very hard to put down.

The last part of the book contains some carefully selected readings that Joseph found when he visited my website in the year 2006. These readings are excerpts from spirit communications that explain the paths that Joseph and his spirit-based family now travel. They are spirit writings from the pen of James E. Padgett that he did between 1914 and 1923. They are not widely known, unfortunately, and Joseph is very skilled in selecting from a large number those that best suit the purpose of his book.

You will not regret reading this book, which I hope is not the last my dear friend, Joseph, will write.

Geoff Cutler
Author – Publisher
Sydney, NSW Australia

# PART ONE

## BEGINNING

## CHAPTER ONE

# CALL FOR MEDIUMS

*"I am here, a stranger, but a spirit interested in the work that you are doing for the Master, and also for many spirits, good and bad."*

These were the first words the medium saw written on the sheet of paper on his desk – written by his own hand by means of a method known as automatic writing. As he did with each message before he began, he dated the message: July 6th, 1915. The name of the medium is James Padgett; the writer of the above message did not immediately give his name – only the words *"I am here, a stranger."*

James Padgett's interest in communicating with spirits developed after his wife died in February of 1914. Soon after this he began to receive messages from his deceased wife and many other spirits. By the time this "stranger" came to write in July of 1915, James Padgett had become a very prolific medium. One of the main writers from the spirit-world that often came to Mr. Padgett is Jesus, who the stranger identifies as the Master.

The message from the stranger continues:

"I am writing by permission of your band, and hence, do not feel that I am intruding. So, if you will kindly bear with me, I will say a few words.

"I am a spirit who loves the efforts that you and your band are making to help the unfortunates who come to you with such pitying tales of suffering and darkness and ask for help. I was once, when on earth, a man who suffered much because of my spiritual darkness, and not until late in life did I find the way to my Father's love through prayer and faith – and even then, I had many erroneous beliefs caused by the interpretations of the Bible, then obtaining in the church of which I was a member. But since coming to the spirit land I have learned the truth, and have gotten rid of any old, erroneous beliefs; and thank God, I am in the way that leads to life everlasting.

"I was a teacher when on earth of what I thought were Bible truths, and I know that some good resulted from my teachings, although they were mixed with errors. But I have since then met many spirits of men who listened to my teachings and believed many things that I taught. So, you see, that even if the churches do teach many false doctrines in their creeds, yet mixed with these false doctrines are many truths, and these truths often find lodgment in the hearts of the hearers, and result in their finding the light and love of the Father.

"I am still teaching mortals whenever it is possible to do. But I find that my task is a difficult one, because there are so few mediums that are capable of receiving the truths of the higher things of life, and the impressions that I make on mortals by the exercise of suggestions are not very encouraging to them or to me. Sometimes the impressions are received and understood, but very often they have no effect.

"If we could have more writing mediums, such as yourself, who are interested in these higher truths, and would believe that we could communicate such truths to them, the salvation of mankind would become much more rapid. But as Jesus said, the harvest is ripe and the laborers are few.

"You have a mission, which is greatly to be envied, I mean in the best sense, because you, by the exercise of your duties, become the medium between the Master and man. And I want to tell you that such a mission is a glorious one and will bring to you untold blessings, because you have now, and will have with increasing power, the influences of the higher world of spirits and angels.

"The one great spirit (I mean the Master) is with you very often and seems to love you so much, and his love and power are beyond comprehension. He is your friend and brother and the association with such a one will give you much spiritual excellence and power, which men have not often possessed. At the same time that this mission holds forth so much glory and power, it also brings with it a great responsibility, and one which will demand of you the exercise of all your love and faith and energy. So, you see with the great favor comes responsibility.

"I have written rather longer than I intended to when I commenced, and I will now stop."

## Comment

It is apparent that James Padgett would not allow the stranger to quit writing until he provided his name. It is not included in the message, but I assume that James asked where he resides in the spirit-world. The stranger answered and wrote:

"I live in the Second Celestial Sphere where your grand-mother and mother and wife live.

"Well, I did not have the love and faith that they had, and my progress was very slow, and hence, they have overtaken me in my spiritual progress. They are wonderful spirits and have so much of the Father's love in their souls.

"I was a preacher and lived the life of one after I separated from the church in which I had been taught the doctrines.

"My name was Martin Luther; yes, Martin Luther, the Monk."

## Comment

I first read the above message from Martin Luther in 2006. I became curious as to whether I could receive messages from spirit. I tried to do automatic writing but found no measure of success with this method and ceased trying.

However, I did not cease altogether: I merely experimented

with other methods. I continued with an interest in exploring the possibility of making a response to Martin Luther's call for more mediums. Thus, after much experimentation, one day I sat at my desk and received a message from Martin Luther.

## Monday – March 3rd, 2014

*"Heavenly Father, you know the desires of our heart before we give expression. And yet you wait for our expressions through our longings and words. You know that I desire to communicate with a Celestial spirit. Today in particular I desire to communicate with Martin Luther. I ask that I be given help to be open to receive what Martin Luther or some other Celestial spirit who may desire to communicate. Thank you, Father."*

### Martin Luther: *"The need for more mediums"*

Yes, Joseph, I am here. I know what it is that you desire to ask, but please proceed and ask. It is important for you to express your words.

*Thank you, Martin. May I call you Martin? Or must I add Luther with Martin? Which do you prefer?*

I am smiling, Joseph, for it is not important, yet, if you publish this, your readers may like to know who it is that is communicating with you.

*Martin, I am pleased to be communicating in this way with you. You are aware that I have been reading the message that you wrote to James Padgett on July 6, 1915. It was the first that you wrote. It was the message where you spoke of the need for more mediums. That was nearly 100 years ago; do you recall?*

Yes, of course I do recall. I also have known that you have a deep interest in writing a book on the subject of mediumship. Is this not correct?

*Yes, this is certainly true. When I read your message, no matter how often I read it, I feel the depth of your call for more mediums. Is this still your concern? Or have you perhaps progressed beyond this concern?*

The subject of mediums to receive our communications is still very much with me. I am as interested today as I was years ago with James Padgett that the message dear to the heart of all Celestial spirits, that people on earth (and in the spirit-world) know about the availability of the Divine Love and how it may transform the soul. We are always endeavoring to assist humans to realize the love that the Father has for all His children. We come to the people of earth and our influence goes only so far. People do respond to our love. Beliefs and fears block further influence. Not too many individuals are willing to break away from their childhood upbringing and other influences as the result of their education (or lack thereof) or their social and family background.

We still look for individuals who are responsive to our call, just as you are endeavoring to do. You are a very reluctant person in this regard. You prefer to take the back seat, as it were. But today we are successful and you have shown willingness to sit and receive our message. I speak in the plural because though you called on me, Martin Luther, there are other Celestial spirits round and about who also desire to speak. You mussel us, although of course you know you cannot fully do this. It is only that you have the ability through your free will to deny us access to our desire to write.

*What you say is very true; I know this about me. I am not one to push myself on anyone. And I do not really like the limelight. Though now, in this moment concerning mediumship and the call for more mediums, I feel a certain amount of responsibility to do this work. As you probably already know, I desire to write and publish a small book on this subject. Are you aware of this?*

Yes, of course, Joseph, I am aware. Where do you suppose your idea originated? The thought has been growing within you because we have been present influencing you in this direction. We hear your prayers; and often you call for Celestial spirits to come and assist you to pray, but you also often call for us to be your continuing influence, your guides and teachers. Is this not true?

*Yes; and I am smiling that you say this. It makes me feel*

*happy to hear confirmation from you. Perhaps I shall then relax and allow you to help me? And then the book will be done! In fact, this morning I jotted a note on a piece of paper, and it was a question: "Communications with Martin Luther?" Did you see me do this?*

[Laughing] I helped you do this! In answer to the other question you wrote (*Would Martin be willing?*) the answer is yes ... I am willing. In fact, Joseph, the idea you wrote in your notes is a good suggestion. Allow this to be the beginning. "Conversations with Martin" has a good ring to it. Let us begin.

*Oh, I wish my fingers could move more quickly on the keyboard! But I like this method better than trying to use automatic writing similar to what James Padgett did.*

Do not be concerned about your method. I am comfortable as I see that you are. After we are done, go back and do your editing and corrections.

Becoming a medium is not mysterious, nor is it a call to a higher realm as some may suppose it to be. All that is required is that a person expresses a desire to do it, to be a vessel willing to sit and write words on paper or through a computer keyboard.

Of course, there must be first a prayer life behind this desire. You are consistent in your prayers Joseph, so this is not an issue with you. For others, they need constant encourage-ment to pray, just as we did with James Padgett. He was an excellent medium and did have certain qualities within his makeup to be an outstanding medium, yet even he required constant prodding to be more in prayer.

When a person begins to develop desires to receive mes-sages from the Celestial spirits, it is best to begin very slowly. Experiment with different methods, whether it is speaking into a machine to record the voice, or whether it is in a prayer group where friends can assist and comment in a loving way. This can be a very effective and immediate transmission that requires no ability to type or write. This is how it was done many years ago in the early gatherings of followers of Jesus.

This same principle applies to writing messages, as you are doing at this moment. You have had some experience with this in years past, but, as I indicated above, you allowed yourself to take a back seat and refused to continue. A related issue with this is that you must have a willingness not be critical and judgmental about what you receive. At times you will mix some of your own ideas and prejudices in with our message; but do not allow criticism to overshadow your work. Go back over what you have written, and with prayer keep what you believe to be from us, and simply delete what you think is your own work. It will all smooth out in the end. In addition, you need to develop confidence in what you receive, and be willing to share it with the world. After all, what we communicate is a benefit not to you alone, but to all mankind.

Now, I want to show you how this works. Take a break and then return. Read what is written. Correct and edit what you see needs correction and editing, and then we will resume our message.

*Well, I did as you suggested; I took a short break for some refreshment. Then I returned and corrected and edited what we had already written. I want to say that on the way to my break I found myself smiling. I was feeling good about our time together and the short writing that we did. While returning to my desk I again smiled, because I felt that I could really do this, namely, sit and write communications with you.*

This is good that you expressed what you have. Some people may feel it cannot be done, but you show that it can be done. You are the proof! Now let me ask: Did you find major changes needing to be made in the writing you did earlier?

*Actually, there were many typing errors, but nothing impossible to fix.*

Good; then we may proceed. I want to speak a short time on the subject of communicating with Celestial spirits.

I know of your interest in communicating with me. It is not just the fact that your desire to communicate with Celestial spirits – but specifically with me. Are you able to articulate why you have this desire?

*This is easy to answer. The simple fact is that I once walked in similar shoes as did you while you were on earth. I am far from an expert about your earthly life; I was not a Lutheran minister, but a Presbyterian one, and then later a Pentecostal minister. So, the affinity I have with your church experience is what draws me to you. And also, the fact that in your message recorded by James Padgett, you said that after you became spirit you continued to teach mortals on earth and discovered it was a difficult thing to do. My desire is to discover in what way I may be of assistance to you; if I am able, I would like to help you.*

Joseph, let us begin by reviewing again what I wrote to James Padgett. Though written in 1915 it is not out of date. Please do this now.

"I was a teacher when on earth of what I thought were Bible truths, and I know that some good resulted from my teachings, although they were mixed with errors. But I have since then met many spirits of men who listened to my teachings and believed many things that I taught. So, you see, that even if the churches do teach many false doctrines in their creeds, yet mixed with these false doctrines are many truths, and these truths often find lodgment in the hearts of the hearers, and result in their finding the light and love of the Father.

"I am still teaching mortals whenever it is possible to do. But I find that my task is a difficult one, because there are so few mediums that are capable of receiving the truths of the higher things of life, and the impressions that I make on mortals by the exercise of suggestions are not very encouraging to them or to me. Sometimes the impressions are received and understood but very often they have no effect.

"If we could have more writing mediums, such as yourself, who are interested in these higher truths, and would believe that we could communicate such truths to them, the salvation of mankind would become much more rapid. But as Jesus said, the harvest is ripe and the laborers are few.

"You have a mission, which is greatly to be envied, I mean in the best sense, because you by the exercise of your duties become the medium between the Master and man. And I want to tell you that such a mission is a glorious one, and will bring to you untold blessings, because you have now, and will have with increasing power, the influences of the higher world of spirits and angels."

Thank you, Joseph. As you and your readers can see, I did try to bring influence by the exercise of suggestions and the results were not good. In all these years we have not seen a response to our influences, except for the fact that individuals are receiving the Divine Love to a degree, and yet they do not know what it is that they have received. The difficulty is to go beyond beliefs created by erroneous doctrines and dogmas and ceremonies. Now, the question is: how to do this?

## Comment

The above message was received by me from Martin Luther on March 3rd, 2014. It was typed and stored with other files in my computer.

Four months passed and I did no further writing. Other interests and personal obligations occupied my time, and the desires to write communications with spirits faded into the background. Then, in July, I returned and wrote the following comment in my journal:

### Sunday – July 6th, 2014

This morning I woke with a desire to communicate with spirit. But first, I felt led to search my documents for things I had written in the past in the area of conversations with spirit.

While browsing files in my computer, I found the previous message from Martin Luther that I had received four months earlier, dated March 3rd. I used the word "found" because, honestly, I completely forgot I had it!

I can accept that I did not remember if I had written it four *years* ago, but how in the world could I forget about it when it was written only a few short months ago? What has been occupying my mind (and heart) these past four months? Yes, I traveled to Australia and this occupied much of my time, and to a degree, expended a great deal of my physical energy. This explains in part my forgetfulness, but I am alarmed that I exhibit a willingness to shun communicating with spirit, and when I do write, forget those I receive. How sad!

I have only a few more minutes to write before I must leave the house. I wonder if Martin may wish to contribute something now. Martin, Martin Luther: are you present and do you desire to respond to my comment?

## Martin Luther: *"Return when you can"*

Joseph, I am not alarmed with your long break from our communication. Be at peace about this; do not criticize and judge yourself. I love you; we all love you.

There is a good lesson to be learned in your recent experience, a lesson both for you and others. We in the Celestial Heavens do not mark time as you on earth do. This being understood, we wait for you (and others) to give yourself the time to sit and receive our communications.

This is much like the Divine Love. The Divine Love waits your active desire to receive it. You are never compelled to do so; and certainly, the Divine Love never forces its way into your soul. To do so would be to disregard your human will.

Yes … We would love to communicate with you, yet, we cannot unless you allow it to take place.

When we begin again, we will begin slowly. This is your choice, Joseph. You have responded to our gentle promptings, and you are present now to take a short note, as it were, from me.

We are here; we are always here. Our voice will not go silent; we will not reject your desire to communicate with us.

Go now; go in peace and with our love. Return when you can. This is in your control. You determine the time and the circumstance; and we will come to help and assist you.

Do your part, though, Joseph: Be at prayer; be vigilant in prayer; be constant in this. For when you receive more of the

Divine Love you will be in the condition necessary to receive our thoughts.

When you are ready, I will come again. Thank you for responding to our promptings and influences. You came today and looked and saw what was started four months ago. Again, do not judge and condemn yourself. We will begin again.

I love you and you are blessed by me and many others, and above all, our Heavenly Father blesses you.

I am Martin – Martin Luther.

## Comment

The call to become a medium was not yet very prominent in my life. I continued to *dabble*, but it is obvious I did not take my work – the call to be a medium – very seriously. Frankly, I was at best *a reluctant scribe* for sprits to write consistently through me.

The story I tell now jumps ahead several months, to the month of November.

## CHAPTER TWO
# I AM AWAKE: DID I DIE?

**PRELIMINARY COMMENT**

I have written a journal of some kind since I was about 20 years-old – sixty-three years ago! There was no thought that I was writing what is known today as journaling. I merely wrote notes, thoughts and experiences, that I felt significant enough to preserve. The notes were not written in a consistent way on same size paper, and my filing system was crude at best. Some notes were merely left in a book that I happen to be reading. Other hand-written notes were saved in a file folder. Many were lost or mistakenly thrown away. Later I was more organized and wrote on 3-ring binder paper, and the binders traveled with me through the years. Of course, a few of these binders were lost when I moved from place to place. Also, I changed with the times; in later years I purchased a computer and wrote many of my writings (dialogues and experiences) using a word program. However, even in the computer age I never completely moved away from writing notes by pen or pencil on paper.

Moving ahead chronologically, in early November of 2014, I picked up the pen again and began to write more frequently in a journal using the old method, namely, writing with a pencil on paper in a notebook.

Incredibly, and certainly with no forethought, something

changed when I began again to write with a pencil on paper. What happened and continues to happen today is quite different than anything I ever experienced in the past.

As already mentioned, I am not new to writing messages from spirits, for I have done this on and off since the mid-1980s. But recently something changed; my writings became so different and new that I do not yet have words to fully describe what it is that I am doing and experiencing.

I am referring to a change that began after I woke one morning with the unshakeable feeling that I had died during the night. I wrote about this experience in my journal, and as the days went on I continued to write each morning. The nature of my writings changed daily; the only way I am able to describe this experience is that I appear to be the observer as well as the active writer.

What follows on the next page are two journal writings – beginning with the experience where I thought that I had died during the night.

Following this, in chapters Three and following, begins the major section of this book: recent spirit communications that I have received beginning in November of 2014. This is where you will read messages from the afterlife that became the breaking of silence – the silence of my own birth family living now beyond the veil, what I call *"Family Reunion"*.

# WRITINGS FROM MY PRIVATE JOURNAL

**Friday – November 7th, 2014**
*"I am awake: Did I die?"*

I am awake!

The lighted clock near my bed read 5:03AM. I feel different. What happened? Did I die during the night? I really mean exactly what I just wrote: *Did I die?*

I am here. I know this ... I need to get up and use the bathroom. It's cold in the house; I feel it and remember that my wife likes warmth when she gets out of bed. She's a school teacher and it is her day to be early at school for playground duty. I walk to the thermostat and turn the furnace on: it responds and rumbles into action.

Did I die? I ask this again because something feels different. What is it? I know I am functioning in this physical body. In this sense, nothing changed. What I just wrote is not quite the truth. I am here; this is true ... yet I am at the same time somehow standing a distance away from my body: close by but feeling that I am observing me. I feel myself standing here but also there. Hardly makes sense. I am aware.

Is it possible to exist in two places at the same time? Here I am feeling present in our bedroom. This physical place feels very heavy and dense. But at the same time, I feel I am further away, existing somewhere less dense, separate, and lighter and feeling very happy.

And then I remember: last evening I whispered a prayer to God: *"Father, if possible, allow me, if you please, to visit during sleep brighter realms of the spirit-world."*

Is this the answer as to why I feel the way I do this morning? Is this why I ask the question: *Did I die during my sleep?*

No; I did not literally die. I do not accept that I died in a literal sense. I did not have what some call *an out of body experience*. Nonetheless, I feel that I did experience heavenly realms during my sleep. I know that I did; yet I cannot recall details of what I saw, experienced and did, and who it was that I spoke with. And yet, I know that the spirit part of who I am visited an extremely beautiful place during my sleep state.

Will this feeling be lost in the shuffle of today's activities?

Will the memory of this experience evaporate just as have all the memories of other places I visited while sleeping? I suppose the answer is: "Somewhat," but not altogether. The beauty of my sleep experience will not completely fade.

I know that I am changed; I am different.

In some measure I did die last night. Part of my physical attachment to this world disappeared. A weight dropped from me. That is why I feel lighter, calmer and very relaxed.

*Heavenly Father: thank you for this experience. Amen.*


## Sunday – November 9th, 2014
### *"Do not hide the real you"*

Today did not begin any differently than yesterday, but somewhere a seed of doubt was planted and I did not see it. Why did I not see that doubt came to my door? This is an easy question to ask, but not as easy to answer.

The doubt that I allowed to be planted grew quickly. I mused about this and that, random thoughts in an attempt to discover the seed of doubt that was beginning to sprout.

After giving expression to my doubt, I was surprised that I became quiet…quiet enough to hear a voice within silence. The voice within said:

"Consider this: You have a unique background, Joseph. Your life began in the church; you were born into it; your father was an ordained minister, and you grew up in the church, both literally and figuratively. You followed your father's footsteps and became a pastor and teacher in the church. Yes, later you walked away from the church, and did a fairly good job of completely disassociating yourself from the church.

"But then in 2006 you read the writings of James Padgett – messages from Jesus and his disciples. You felt unusually drawn to these messages, even after you saw traces of the church in them. You stayed with these messages, studied them and even took time to publish them in the date order in which James received them.

"Well, you are not being forced to proceed further. You are a free man.

"Consider your true feelings. You are not feeling happy. In fact, you are feeling lost: 'floundering' is the word that you used."

Then I spoke and said: *"What am I to do? What is the next step for me?"*

The voice within spoke again:

"You know the answer. I come only to remind you. Go to God in prayer, Joseph: enter into your closet of prayer. Wait upon God: wait upon the Father. Wait, seek, ask and knock.

"This has been your way in past years whenever you experienced doubt. Be who you are; Joseph. Do not attempt to be anyone else but you. You have come this way because this is you. Thus, I do plead with you to see clearly: Do not bury or attempt to hide the real you. Not now; not ever."

Then I responded: *"I agree ... this is me. You are not forcing me. I go willingly. I will stop now; I write no more. I go now to pray!"*

**Later the same day – November 9th, 2014**

I went to my prayer closet. Please don't take this literally! I have no such closet. When I pray I usually sit or recline in a soft arm chair in my office – but, sometimes not. On occasion

I will go outdoors to walk in the forest. Today I felt like sitting in my recliner.

When I began my prayer, it was almost immediate: I cried, I sobbed; yes, I even raised my voice to a loud noise. It doesn't need to be this way, and it is not usually. But today it seemed a good thing to do. I poured out my heart-feelings to my Father – God who is our Heavenly Father, and He felt the energies of my heartbeat.

God is not deaf that He cannot hear even our most silent prayer. Nor is He uneasy with the noise we may make or the tears we may shed. He hears the cry of His children, for we are the children of His care, and the objects of His Great Soul Love and most tender care.

We are not wayward children that He waits to scold and punish with a firm rod of chastisement. He is not an angry and vengeful God, ready to devour us in a fire of anger.

God is our Loving Heavenly Father. God is Love. He loves us individually and is always ready to help us and take us into His waiting arms of love.

I experienced all the above and more when I went to God in prayer. My soul felt cleansed. I was changed and am continually being changed by the presence of His Love. His love surrounds me, envelopes me, and is available to enter the depths of my soul – that is, IF I will allow it. God has given us free will, and therefore I have the right of refusal. I am free to reject His Love. He never forces His Love upon me or anyone. We are free to walk away and go a direction of our own choosing.

I cried to God with a heavy heart, and a voice whispered to me: *"I am here, I am always here: forever. I will always be here. You are one of my beloved children. You are the focus of my attention. When you are ready, when you determine the right time, you will find that I am here and already waiting. I am ready, always ready; I am waiting here for you. Speak and I will hear. Come to me; my arms of love are waiting for you. Taste and see that My Love is real and genuine. You are the one to determine if you want to experience my Love. You make the choice. My love for you is waiting."*

After this, I paused a long time in quietness. Then the voice from the quiet place within spoke to me again:

"Happy are you when you awake to the realization of exactly how close the Father's Love is to you and to each and all His children.

"Now, Joseph, tell me, speak to me of the change you feel."

"Father, Heavenly Father, I feel calm. I am happy; I am smiling. I feel connected. I feel harmony – harmony with myself and who I am. I feel balanced. And I feel like singing – singing a happy song, a song of healing, release and joy.

"I have been through a battle, a battle of my soul, and I have come through to the other side with scars; yet I am free of pain and will celebrate the victor's song."

## Call to Rejoice

"Come everyone and join with me in a time of feasting and celebration, for I was desperately ill with a disease of self-loathing and feelings of rejection and despair. But I went to my Father – our Heavenly Father, and He heard my cry and saw my pain; He wiped away my tears with His Great Love. I gave tears and He gave Love – His Divine Love, and now it resides in my soul as abiding grace Divine.

"Come let us be glad and rejoice together in the Presence of such Love."

CHAPTER THREE
# MESSAGES FROM THE AFTERLIFE

## Monday – November 10th, 2014

*I am up early today. Rather than write, I decide to pray.*

*Prayer was 'light' – meaning that the experience was quiet, mostly silent, with feelings of softness. I recognized the Presence of Love and welcomed the presence of friends in spirit, bright spirits of the Celestial Heavens. Today I accept and embrace my identity as a child of God; I am loved, I am sustained by Love; I am being changed by Love.*

*Today I feel that I would like to entertain a spirit-friend and invite one to speak through pen and paper. I ask: Is there a Celestial friend who would like to write a message this morning? If the answer is yes, then I ask for your help to make this possible ... So, I wait.*

## Martin Luther: *"Your voice is needed"*

Yes, Joseph, I come with your invitation to write.

You will not have the words before you begin. The words that will appear will come as you place the pen on the paper. Merely allow this to happen. Do not attempt to control the flow. Do not search for a word to write. You may certainly correct and edit when you feel we are finished.

Let us begin. You are concerned about the work you may

have remaining to do before you transition. Be assured that your transition will not happen any day soon. So, I urge you to find your peace about this concern. When you do then you will discover that you are relaxed and calm.

Your voice is needed; I and many others desire to assist you to find your voice. We understand your surprise; nonetheless, it is true. There is a company of us; we are many. We are your friends and are close – nearly constantly – helping and guiding you. We desire to assist you to become a voice to others on earth. The individuals present with me are many; most of us were once preachers and teachers on earth, as you yourself once were. Our names are for the most part very familiar to you. I am Martin – yes, Martin Luther. Standing near are many others; one will bring surprise to you, for he is your own father, Andrew. There are many others too; in proper time their names will be revealed to you.

Our message to you now is that we are being very careful and, as it were, very delicate with you. We tell you this because, though you are in many ways a very strong individual, with determination and resolve; yet, you also possess a tendency to self-defeat and feel easily hurt. You often interpret the latter as weakness and unworthiness. When you become more successful in the acceptance of your purpose and potentialities, growing in your experience of the Father's Love changing and assisting you, then you will be our voice in the world – not only to mankind, but more specifically, our voice to Christianity and to present-day church leaders.

This will be no easy task. Often, we have tried this with other individuals but they resisted. To some extent you also have resisted, but, of course, for different reasons as mentioned above.

The beginning of your work will be of necessity slow. We are aware of your recent contact with a church leader (TB_). You knew her many years ago, and it is good that you are restoring your connection with her. Another person is your friendship with DS_, and his connection with a group in TN. We hope that he will respond positively to your contact. There are others; we will bring their names and places to your attention. Are you willing? We will not force you to do this work; but we sincerely invite you to be our voice.

We are aware of your present position. We would not ask if we knew you lack abilities to do what we ask you do. All that we ask is your willingness.

Presently you are hesitant. This is to be expected. It is all new to you, and we are aware. We say now that the plan and purpose is very large. You will not be alone. We are with you now and promise to be with you each day and each step of the way. We are your friends in spirit, but there are also others on earth, and they will be made known to you.

You ask: will it be a book? Will it involve speaking engagements? You also wonder if the work will include visits to churches and theological schools. All this may be possible; but at this time, we will not share the specific plans. These and other things will be shown when the time is appropriate. Again, remember what we said at the beginning of our message: we begin slowly.

Our rapport is weakening. We will close. With all our love, we are your friends and we are One.

Martin – Martin Luther, with many others.


## Wednesday – November 12th, 2014

*I woke early again today. In my office I read various emails ... and then to prayer.*

*Prayer again was rich; I am feeling very grateful. Emphasis on the fact that the Divine Love is not about religion, dogma or doctrine, but about individuals and their experience with God. My specific prayer at this moment is that I be open to a spirit communicating with me. I wait ...*

## Martin Luther: *"A new Pentecost"*

Good morning, Joseph; yes, it is your friend Martin – Martin Luther.

We are all here; we were pleased to be with you as you prayed. We love the prayer that Jesus gave, and we enjoy the experience of joining with you as you pray this prayer. The way that you pray is never the same; it shows that you have not made a ritual of prayer, and it is not mere recitation.

We are aware of your concern when you shared the message we gave to you two days ago, and that you shared it with your friend. We wish to say that we are pleased that you did this. We are happy to know that he shared it with others, for the core of that message is that the call to individuals is going forth, and his response was positive. It is confirmation that you are not singled out as the sole voice of Celestial spirits.

You are one of many, and we acknowledge you have a sense of relief, and that you appreciate this clarification. There are many others on earth that are responding to the call from Celestial spirits, and we are happy that you are among those on earth responding to our call.

Nonetheless, Joseph, do not be hasty. We want you to feel free to share our messages as you will. Yet, we ask you to be attentive: Look and observe, study and become more aware of the evidence of the multitude of ways that we Celestial spirits are giving voice to the movement of the Father's Spirit to bring the message of the Divine Love to light – to the awareness of increasing numbers of people on earth responding to the Presence of Love – the Divine Love. Open your eyes and ears and you will behold a wonderful thing happening on earth at this time.

We have observed how you responded to our message of a few days ago. Your response is evidence of our continuing presence and influence.

Yes, you are correct in that you sense the call to prepare for a new Pentecost. However, we are not looking to gather people to one specific location – to an assembly in a building of any sort. The call we are issuing is not to a church or a conglomerate of churches; our call – the Father's call – is to individuals throughout the world.

It is a call to individuals to respond to the promptings in their heart to the presence of love. The feelings people are experiencing are real. It is a call to be open to the influence of Love; it a call to receive Love, to accept it and allow it to flow freely into the soul. Our desire is to see individuals begin to feel loved and accepted by their Creator – our Heavenly Father.

It is the time to experience the true essence of brotherhood and the importance and worth of each and every individual on earth.

You will assist us in this effort; your voice will help; you will join with the voices of many people who know what is happening and are telling other people what it is they are experiencing has its source in heavenly places.

This is the new Pentecost, Joseph; it is reaching out beyond the walls of sectarianism and religious institutions representing hundreds of conflicting doctrines and dogmas. This new Pentecost is the breaking down of the walls of separation that have been constructed and divided humanity into thousands of separate groups.

The Spirit of Love cannot be institutionalized, nor can it be bottled into separatist groups. Our Father's Love is for the individual human soul; it is for each and all of us – humans on earth and spirits of mortals once on earth and now living in the spirit-world.

This is not my voice alone that is assisting you to write these words. I am Martin Luther along with many preachers of old; we are many voices. Yes, even our beloved Master is present – Jesus our elder brother and friend; he also is attending the writing of this message. The call to humanity is originating from the Celestial Heavens, and it is intended, not just for your ears alone, it is intended for all humanity on earth.

Allow the message to go out into the world. May all that see it respond and expand the work of making known the Presence of God's Great Love to all on earth today.

Broadcast this message to as many as possible. The Spirit of the Father is moving throughout the world; each and every individual is being visited. This is the word that must go forth. Do what you are able to do. Do not hold back; do not hide the word. What we give to you, give to others. Encourage those that listen and hear to do the same.

The Master says: *"The Father's Love is reaching out to all the world; the Divine Love is waiting for each and all."* Help others to see and realize the truth of this. Not one person is excluded. Divine Love is for all people everywhere.

We have written enough for now. Blessings to you, and to

all who read our messages – Martin Luther.

## Friday – November 14th, 2014

*I am very distracted today. I was up very early (3:00AM). I cannot recall what I did; only to say I experienced many distractions. Time in prayer was very short, and during prayer I felt very restless. It is now three hours later and I will be surprised if a Celestial desires to write.*
*I wait ...*

## Philip: *"Distraction"*

I am here... You are very correct in saying that you have been distracted. I will not write long.

I do want to encourage you as you develop thoughts and ideas how to begin to speak to people about the message of the Divine Love. We spoke to you about not being too hasty. This advice applies to your contact with "outsiders" – to those who have no knowledge whatsoever of the existence of the Divine Love.

The idea you have of the 'storyteller' is a good beginning. Many of your thoughts, ideas and feelings are the true evidence of the presence of your guides. You can trust them. This explains to some extent the restlessness that you experienced this morning. It is the expression of your wrestling with this or that thought.

This will settle down. Do not be alarmed, and certainly do not criticize yourself. This morning was not wasted time. You were right not to force your prayers, especially not making it a forced ritual and something you must do. Your soul longings for the Divine Love have been heard and Divine Love has been received into your soul, whether you felt the evidence of it or not. This is where your practice of trust enters the picture.

You ask: were Celestial spirits present Wednesday evening at the program where the leader led a program to "Ask the Angels." But of course! Your presence was appreciated. Because you were there, the leader is now curious about you.

She was pleased as were the others in attendance.

If you attend again, and we urge you to return, you may ask the angel about us, and what the leader's guide see. We will lead you what to ask. And be sure that you attend the program in December at the public library. Be prepared to speak about your experience discovering the Padgett messages back in 2006. Your story will fit well with the program theme: *Have you had a spiritual experience?* You have ideas about handing out small cards telling about your books. These are small steps and we encourage you to take them. Everything has its beginning. The long walk always begins with the first small step. So, it is with the work you are being called to do.

*Who is this writing today?*

My name is Philip. I am with others, of course. Yes, Martin Luther is here, as is your father, Andrew, and many others. Take a break; we will resume later.

## Comment

The message from Philip was comforting and also disturbing. I always find it comforting to receive a message from a Celestial angel.

The disturbing part is this: Why was the name of my biological father given at the end? This disturbed me a great deal. What purpose did this serve?

I did take a break but did not return to continue Philip's message.

Perhaps I did not return because my father was mentioned by Philip as also present. I am perplexed with my response. Martin Luther mentioned my father in the message that he gave on November 10th and I did not have a similar response. At that time, Martin's mention of my father went unnoticed: why?

*Are the angel-friends preparing me for something?*

## Saturday – November 15th, 2014

*I feel better! It is nearly 7AM and I have been up since 2AM. I have been feeling very troubled about a very small detail – a name or title I plan to create later today for a business card. I've bounced around with two ideas ("Conversations with Joseph" and "Storytelling with Joseph"). Neither seem appropriate. I do see myself presenting stories and conversations to small groups of people, but I do not like this as the introduction or the theme of public presentations. I see myself "Sharing News of God's Great Love." This is why I feel good. I feel that my guides helped me to see this. It actually happened shortly after I began to pray this morning. Then I fell asleep in my recliner for nearly two hours, and when I woke the same words were still with me. Do my Celestial friends wish to comment about this?*

## Martin Luther: *"The only solid remedy"*

Good morning, Joseph –

We are here and pleased to say that we are happy with your development. Yesterday you were conflicted about the thought of making yourself available for public talks. This was the exhibit of recurring doubts, which you often translate into feelings of unworthiness. These feelings do not begin with your thought of being unworthy, but rather in your relationship with the Father, and also us – your Celestial friends.

As we continue in our conversations these feelings will appear again, but with experience they will fade and may even disappear, dependent on the continuing development of your soul with your acceptance of the Divine Love. Prayer and sincere longings for the Father's Love is the only solid remedy. You know this intellectually, and you are learning this experientially daily.

This, what you are doing now, is part of our plan for you. You are beginning with small steps, and these first steps will lead you into bigger things. This is much like the photo you are considering using for the cover of your book. The things you are doing, and now planning, picture the steps you took when you were recovering from the auto accident years ago.

Today you cannot see where your present steps will lead tomorrow or the next month and even the next year. As Philip told you, every journey begins with the first small step.

We do suggest that you follow through with your latest decision concerning the small business card. This will be well received. It will be a good introduction of you as a speaker, and of us, the writers of the messages we gave to James Padgett. So now you may be able to see why there is such a large company of Celestial spirits interested in you, your work and your success.

We like what you wrote to your friend that you desire to be a servant of the Padgett Messages. This is a very high desire on your part; we want you to realize that we will be with you, right alongside you, as you strive to be faithful to this desire.

May God our Heavenly Father bless you abundantly with His Love – is our prayer for you.

We are one – your Celestial friends,
Martin Luther with many others.


**Tuesday – November 18th, 2014**

*I woke early again today and prayed earnestly. Prayers with Father and Celestial spirits were rich and full ... using as usual the free-form use of the beautiful prayer that Jesus gave to James Padgett. I paused long and silently "in the arms of our Father's Love."*

*After this I went to my desk, wrote the above words in my journal and then paused and wrote: Is there a Celestial friend present who may desire to write? I wait ...*

**An unlikely visitor**

Good morning dear Joseph; I am here, your father –

Yes, I see your smile – and yet I see that you are doubtful that it is truly I, your earthly, biological father. I have progressed a great deal since I passed so long ago. It is difficult for you to take my message. Let this first message be brief, then, for it may take time for you to realize that I truly am your father. I shall return – if you will permit this.

## Comment

I feel overwhelmed with a variety of feelings.

I was taken by surprise when I saw the words on paper and that the writer purported to be my dad. I felt a rush of displeasure and anger. Why would he come at this time, during a period when I have only just begun to feel relaxed with the idea of communicating with spirits?

I was only a sixteen-year-old boy when my father died. I disliked him a great deal and went through much pain to accept my feelings and overcome them. Healing was slow.

Why did he come and write today? Why did my guides allow this to happen? What purpose does his presence have?

I am perplexed: my father sensed this and broke off writing. Or was it I who would not allow him to write more?

I did not feel closed to further writing, but I did not feel I could or would like to receive a message from my dad.

So, breathing deeply, I wait again …

## Later the same day – November 18th, 2014

*I gave myself time and space to think, meditate and pray about the brief message that I received from my father. When I felt ready, I went to my desk again to write ...*

## Martin Luther: *"Be open and awake"*

Joseph, this is your friend Martin –

I understand your feelings surrounding the visit of your father. In time you will relax and welcome his presence. He will return to write soon. Andrew is a loving spirit and loves you very much. Yes, it is true that he has his home in the Celestial Heaven, and this is also true of your mother. She will come and write you also; this will be for another day. There is a purpose behind Andrew coming to you now; this purpose will be revealed as we continue with our messages.

I would like to share that we are all pleased with your progress, not only with us and receiving our messages, but with your progress as you begin your public work.

The business card that you created is but a small step. It expresses well your desire to be of help to the cause of making known the truth of the Divine Love. Your public presence will grow.

Prepare a place where people may come and hear you speak about your experience of the Divine Love. We will show this to you as you continue responding to our help and influence. We will give you suggestions along the way as you are taking steps in the direction you feel led to go.

Do not be anxious about having a place to meet. This will come. Perhaps you will meet at the public library. Be open to what develops. An individual who attends the same meeting where you will be in December may have a suggestion for you. Listen to clues and promptings. Does this not sound exciting?

It is a new day for you; it is a new beginning. Be open and awake to what is developing in your life. All that is happening is an unfolding experience. Do not attempt to get ahead of what is taking place; do not be in a rush; do not attempt to force this or that to happen.

Do not run when a slow walk is required. Above all things, be open and awake to what is presented before you. Listen and observe the signs that are being presented.

We are present and we will help you along the way, even to the extent of what to say when you begin your public appearances. The following is a suggested outline of subjects:

• Awareness of the existence of the Celestial Messages: This will be first.

• Your personal experience will be next.

• And third, an invitation to listeners to participate in the experience of the presence of Love.

These three things will be your focus. But how they will be presented will change and evolve. We urge you to be open to this brief outline. It must not be static or dogmatically presented. You must not be stern, inflexible, dogmatic and static. Be gentle and open to the individuals you will meet. With loving eyes, see each person as a unique individual, a precious child of God.

This will be enough for now. We will speak again.
We are your Celestial friends and guides. We are one.
I am Martin Luther, with many others.

## Wednesday – November 19th, 2014

*Today I woke at 3:30AM ... Prayer at 4:30am, which was very calm, expressing appreciation for continuing guidance and help from Celestial friends, and the blessings of our Heavenly Father's Love.*
*I feel that I want to communicate with my dad, Andrew.*
*So, I wait ...*

## Andrew: *"Connecting with family again"*

Yes, Joseph, my son, I am here, your father –
*Thank you for returning again to write. I want to apologize for my actions yesterday. I was surprised how I reacted and responded to your presence. I could not really accept that it was you, really you, and I confess that I felt anger toward you. How can I truly know this is not my imagination? Is there some way that I may know?*
Let me respond, my son. I am aware of your feelings toward me. After all, consider that we did not communicate much, practically none, and you were so young when I passed. I did not pass in good condition, and I was a long time recovering.

I was bewildered and confused when I first awoke in spirit. Yes, it required a very long time for me to adjust to my new surroundings. I will tell you a more complete story of my progression later; I will tell only a few details today.

You will be happy to hear that your beloved brother, Charles, was present when I woke. He looked so very happy to see me! We did cry, for I too loved him, and we all were crushed when we heard news of his death during the war. Well, his appearance was beautiful, and he had such a happy countenance about him. He smiled nearly continuously. I was curious of course what the source of his happiness was.

Charles helped me, his own father, and I was in his care and charge. He was my guide and showed me his beautiful home and the wonders of my new life here. Others were also present to help me adjust to my passing.

Later, after I had been in the spirit-world for a time, I took a keen interest in you, as did Charles. Oh, we did not only concentrate on you alone, for there were at that time many of our family still on earth. This was all before your mother passed. She will come to tell you of her experience.

We were drawn to you; you were of special interest to us because we saw your potential and also your stubbornness. This latter quality was unusual; it was not a negative thing, though it could have been. This stubbornness allowed you to be critical and not mere acceptant of what life put before you. In other words, you were willing to question and, if needed, change and move in other directions, which you did often and in some measure are still doing. I am not your primary guide, Joseph. You had and now have several guides. Perhaps it would help you to see that I was a very interested bystander, and at times, when asked by your guides, to provide direct help.

You are still asking whether I am truly your father that is communicating in this way with you. I offer this for your consideration, it is this: It was I who was present this morning and impressing you with my name. It was I who was present when Philip suggested to you that I was with him while he was writing.

Yes, you may call me dad or Andrew if you so choose. Either will be fine. You have a longing that I write you, and I want to say that I am very anxious that you allow me to do this. I will not force you, and I will not be bothersome, for I am aware of your present interests and activities.

Charles would like the opportunity to write, as would your mother; she is of such beautiful radiant presence...and of course all the family, which you know, are now many. They want you to know that they are all quite fine and happy in their life here.

You are correct, we are not all together in one location, and we certainly are no longer what you know as 'family'. We each have our separate lives; we are individuals. I am no longer a father to them – or the husband of Julia, your mother. We are more like friends, if you can accept this. Yes, your sister, Margie, and I now get along quite nicely. She is no longer bitter toward me, nor is your brother, Bundy. Each one of us is progressing, some faster than others; but all are happy in their own way and in their own space and experience.

I sense that your feelings have already changed from the experience you had with my unexpected visit yesterday. In days ahead, you will see this as an important experience for you, for you discovered that you still had ill feelings toward me. Because you are older and have the perspective that comes with years, and because you also have a good amount of the Divine Love, family injuries have been removed to a large extent. I had these same injuries, as did your brothers and sisters.

When you discovered the Divine Love while reading James Padgett's writings (yes, I have met James) you changed, shall we say, explosively. And when you had this experience, all of us already in the spirit-world benefited. I am not suggesting it was the time that I discovered the Divine Love; no. Not long after I passed into the spirit-world, very kind and helpful spirits showed me the truth of the Divine Love, and similar to your experience, I almost immediately embraced the teachings of the Way of Divine Love. It became my salvation, and I progressed fairly quickly.

Yes, I had many of the same injuries as you and had a hard time releasing them. I was stagnant, and when the teachings of the Divine Love were introduced to me I began to experience change and transformation. When I saw your response, as you read the writings of James Padgett, I felt gratefulness and happiness. And now whenever I see and hear you pray the way that you do, this adds to my joy; *it also helps us when we listen to your prayers.* Some of the spirits here that attend your prayer time are your own kin. This is true, Joseph, and I know that you feel the truth of what I am telling you.

This has become quite a long message. It was good writing you like this. I pray we may do this again soon.

I realize your family awaits your assistance. Go, my son. We will communicate again. We cannot say everything that needs to be said in one message. I have thoroughly enjoyed my time with you. I love you, my son and my friend. Yes, I am your friend.

With all the love and blessings of our Heavenly Father,

I am Andrew – your father when I was on earth long ago.

## BACKGROUND INFORMATION

Andrew Babinsky, my biological father, was born in 1887 in Hungary. He attended a small college and became a teacher and immigrated to the United States in 1911. He met Julia Kayati in 1914 and married soon after. They had twelve children, and I was their last child. Andrew was diagnosed with cancer in 1949 and suffered a very long and painful illness. He died at home on October 2, 1951. My mother attended to his nursing, as did my sister, Margie. Andrew was an ordained Christian minister; at the time of his death he was the pastor of the Hungarian Evangelical and Reformed Church located in the Riverside section of Buffalo, New York.

When my father died, I was a sixteen-year-old boy and it affected me deeply. I had not resolved my angry feelings toward him. The resolution of anger came later in my life, yet I was surprised these feelings surfaced again when he first came to write the day previous. The anger I felt was real, but it was no longer deep-seated. Thus, I was able to return the next day with a sincere desire to communicate again with my father.

It was good for me to experience this connection through spirit communications. However, the reader must realize that at this point in the story I had no expectation beyond the fact of the initial contact with my father.

### Additional Reflections

It has been six days since I last recorded a message from spirit. It is the holiday season, which is always a busy time in our home.

I feel somewhat different since I heard from my dad. I shared his message over the telephone with my sister, Marie.

She cried while I read it. She and I talked about it after I finished reading. I mentioned my reluctance to fully accept that this was not my imagination. She helped me to see that it was not. I am happy that I shared it with her. It will make it easier to share with others who are not family.

In his message on Tuesday, November 18th, Martin said this: *"There is a purpose behind Andrew coming to you now; this purpose will be revealed."* That is already happening. I have not sat to receive another message from spirit, but the feeling of the presence of spirits is more real than it has ever been prior to my father coming to write.

When I reflect on this, I wonder what it felt like to James Padgett to have his wife and other family members come so close to him. These experiences had to help him accept the presence of Jesus and other Celestial spirits. And not only this, but it also helped James accept the presence of the Father's Great Love.

Divine Love can be experienced as being more real than anything in all of nature. It is not a mere intellectual assertion, but rather, a verifiable thing by and through our experience.

I am grateful for my recent experiences.

### Saturday – November 29th, 2014

*I have not written a message in over a week and I don't feel guilty or negligent. This is new for me. Today I feel somewhat anxious as I anticipate a Celestial friend to come near to write. I pray that I am open and in relatively good condition to receive a message from spirit. I feel that I am, and now I wait to see who shall come to write...*

### Jesus: *"It is time"*

I am here, and I desire to give a message –

Yes, I realize that you did not pray in your usual way – which at times can be very long. But you did have true soul longings for the Divine Love which, as you know, is faster than formed thought, and sufficient for the Father to hear and answer.

You have the thought that it is your elder brother, Jesus, who writes this, and you are correct. I have not had the opportunity like this in a very long time, and I do have a message for you and your friends.

"*It is time.*" These three words were spoken by your friend Geoff during the recent Divine Love Retreat in Washington, DC. I am happy that you attended this gathering. It is time for all my friends on earth to reach out in a host of ways to mankind with the message and demonstration of the availability of the Divine Love.

Many persons are having experiences that are directly related to the Divine Love, and yet they have neither knowledge nor awareness about what it is that they are experiencing. You and all others who are aware the Divine Love exists and know something of its purpose and effect in human lives, must begin reaching out to these individuals to help them realize that it is God's Great Love that they are experiencing. Love, the Divine Love, is the only answer.

Joseph, it is time for you to make yourself known in your community, and to do this you must make yourself available and accessible. Martin Luther has been guiding you and your response has been good. This coming week will be the time to begin your public appearance. We will be present to assist you. You will not know the particulars of our help until you are present at the meeting on Saturday. At this time, today, as you are writing this message, what we are saying is only a very small fraction of the influence you will feel one week from today. I am as anxious as you are.

We will not force our presence upon those attending the meeting, yet, to those who will be open, they will feel something uniquely different. When you speak you will have clear vision of the change that came to you when you began to read our messages to mankind given to James Padgett. What you say will have influence with listeners because we will be present to each one.

They will remember and some will even express a desire to hear more about your experiences. With our presence and influence it will be a memorable event for many. Please remember that we will not exert pressure in order to force their attention. Hungry souls will open to our presence. This is all that I need to say at this time about the meeting that you will attend next week Saturday.

I want to encourage you to continue being open and willing to record messages from your Celestial friends. I am happy that your own father, Andrew, came to write and to be a member of the band of helpers assisting you at this time. Andrew's presence has given you deeper confidence in the work we have planned for you to do. Your mother and others in your family are also present to encourage you. Our task is not easy, for you are not one to quickly step forward into the public eye, but we see that you will.

I come to encourage you and all who read this message, that each person with the Divine Love has a similar work as Joseph. He is not singled out. Each person is called to speak of your experience in receiving God's Love. Do not be afraid or hesitant, for Celestial angels are with you.

It is time that each one does his or her part in fulfilling the desire of our Heavenly Father that all His children everywhere hear the Good News about Divine Love, and the possibility of the transformation of the human soul. Our prayer and hope are that others will see your personal transformation. Your family, neighbors and friends will notice the change happening in your life, so do not be shy. Tell them exactly what it is that is making the great change in your life.

You have received a good portion of the Divine Love. Some of you have been enjoying this process for many years. As you step out in faith you will experience even greater inflowing of the Father's Great Love.

The light of Divine Love is within you and it cannot be hid. You have the truth and *you are the truth*: it is within you. It is the Divine Love, the substance of our Heavenly Father's Great Soul.

Relating to matters of receiving the Divine Love, you realize that only you can prevent this love from changing you into a Divine Angel on earth. Your life is now about the Divine Love revealing its transforming power in your life, so that others may see and cause them to wonder what this change is that they see in your life. Only you can prevent the visibility of the Divine Love in your life. Do not attempt to hide this from others.

*It is time* – the right time to allow the manifestation of the light of Divine Love in you to shine in all the dark places in your world.

Well, I have written enough; it is a long message for you to record.

Let me close then, by saying this to all: Be who you are – the beloved sons and daughters of your loving Heavenly Father. We are all His children; we are all the objects of His Great Love and most tender care. His Love, the Divine Love, is waiting for everyone.

With the Love and Blessings of the Father, and my love and blessing,

I am your brother and friend,

Jesus.

## Sunday – November 30th, 2014

*I did not really want to pray today. Instead I did meaningless work on my computer. In addition, I did not want to send the messages that I have received from spirit to various friends for their review. I felt that the messages would be merely seen as works of my active ego. Truthfully, I was feeling low: Feelings of unworthiness and despair were hitting me like high waves at the ocean.*

*Finally, I realized what was happening and I determined to go to pray. If I have learned anything these past several years, I have learned to recognize negative influences, and not to give power to them. So, I went to prayer.*

*The time in prayer was filled with power through energetic expressions of body, mind and soul. Prayer brought another victory for the soul: The victory is the celebration of the Divine Love, the greatest thing in all the world.*

*God and His beautiful Divine angels cannot do this work for us. Love and peace await us, but they cannot be our experience without the action on our part that they be our*

*possession. I go to the Source: the Father's Love, and I find again that it has been present all along. I am the one who allows clouds to come and hide God's Love. As a result, I become weak and doubts assail me. The remedy remains always the same: Go to God in prayer!*

*I did this and now I celebrate the victory. The victory that I celebrate is that I once again experienced the flow of our Father's Love.*

*And now I feel free to ask: Is there a spirit who may like to write a message? I wait...*

### John: *"Give as an offering of love"*

Yes, I am here, John, one of your friends –

I want to say only this:

Send the messages you have received to your friends. Broadcast them. Freely you have received, freely give. Give the messages as an offering of love.

Do not worry how you think the messages will be received by others. If some people reject the messages, do not take it personally.

The messages you are receiving are expressions of your soul progression. They are not final documents: they are not the final word from spirit on any subject. The messages you receive are evidence of the path you have taken.

I am John, one of your helpers.

Yes, I am here with Martin Luther and others.

### Comment

As the result of what John wrote above, and other recent spirit communications, I gathered messages that I had received and sent them to friends for them to read and review.

I did not receive a single negative comment. Instead, and to my surprise, I received positive responses that showed appreciation. This gave me courage to continue with my work. Shortly after this I made a decision to include these messages in a new book.

## Monday morning – December 8th, 2014

*Heavenly Father, here I am. I am feeling much better now that I have prayed and experienced the Presence of Your Love. Love – Divine Love – always makes life here on earth much better!*

*This weekend was unusual, to say the least. I pray that my spirit friends and counselors are with me now and listening to what I am saying. I felt very happy on Saturday when I met with people who came to the program at the Public Library on the subject "Have you had a spiritual experience?" There were 16 people present. It seemed to me that most already knew each other. We sat in a circle and each took a turn telling a personal experience of a spiritual nature. I was the next to the last person to speak. I shared a brief account of my personal journey to the Padgett Messages. Looking back, I feel that I talked too much about me and not enough about the messages that James received. Did I even mention the Father's Great Gift of Love? Did I mention that Jesus was the main writer of the hundreds of messages that James recorded? I hardly remember anything that I said.*

*Enough now of me – I so much want to hear from Spirit. I anxiously wait. I pray: If I am open to receive a message, I wait.*

## Hugh Taggart: *"Encouragement"*

I am here, Taggart, yes, Hugh Taggart –

I see that you are surprised: yes, it is indeed your friend, Taggart.

We feel your pain – unwarranted as it is. Many of us were present, trying our best to help you, also to help those who were present. Yes, it may be true that you could have spoken differently by giving more direct reference to the subject of the Divine Love, but please understand, this may have caused a shock to ripple among the listeners and closed a door of opportunity to speak again. I tell you, you did well my friend; be assured of this. Individuals are now curious about you. They see something different about you. A seed was planted and now it must be watered.

I just wanted to say this and want to thank you for allowing me to write.

Yes, I am often with you. I was first attracted to you because of the love that you have expressed toward me as the result of reading my experiences written by my friend, James Padgett.

I would like to write again sometime. Yes, I am a Celestial spirit, and have been a very long time. Others are waiting to write, so I must close.

I am your friend,

Hugh Taggart.

## Martin Luther: *"Encouragement"*

This is Martin, yes, Martin Luther –

We thought you would enjoy a message from Hugh Taggart. I am glad it was a happy surprise for you.

We are happy with your activity these last few days. Continue to be patient; as we have said, do not rush ahead of yourself with imaginations as to what could have been said, neither judge yourself for what you think you actually said. I do not feel that you have an accurate recollection of what you did indeed share. Curiosity is even now growing in the feelings and thoughts of those who heard you speak. That you returned the next day to attend their "church" service delighted many.

You have the thought to correspond with several people you met and I encourage you to do this. This will help you and also them. When you do this, mention a few people who have had similar experiences of God's Love. Some may enjoy reading the message from John Yorking about the early church.

The idea that you have of securing a meeting room at the Public Library is excellent. Perhaps individuals that you met at the meeting may help by publicizing your meetings. Follow through and do it; plan ahead and be open to possibilities.

This will not be a long message today. We only want to encourage you and support your work. We are with you. Yes, I was present both Saturday and Sunday. Yes, we helped you when you had an unusual coughing spell. That was caused by a brief intrusion of a lower spirit, attempting to cause you to be distracted. For a moment it worked, but do you not remember how quickly the physical symptoms disappeared? And do you recall that shortly after this incident you had a personal message given to you?

All the messages given to individuals by channelers during the Sunday meeting were genuine; although good, none were from high spirits. The low spirits sensed our presence but did not know what to make of us. Let me ask, did you notice and remember how often the various speakers used the word 'light'? This was the direct result and evidence that we were there.

Continue to pray and to write. There is much that we have to share with you. As your spiritual condition improves we will be here with you to teach and guide you. Be of good cheer. Again, we say, do not judge the words you spoke and the activity of your work.

You are a blessing to others. Believe this and continue to be humble. Your humility will be the way the blessings that come to you will flow toward others and become their personal experiences of love. You are not the source of the love; you are like a vehicle allowing the blessings of love to be present.

I will close now. If you feel able to do so, there are others here that wish to write. Perhaps take a short break and return for their messages.

I am your friend, and I bless you with love as does your Heavenly Father,

Martin Luther.

## Andrew: *"Encouragement"*

Good morning, Joseph, I am your father who writes –

I want to say how all of us are very proud of you. Perhaps I am the only one present who can use this word and have so much meaning for you. I am indeed very proud. You are doing well to go out into the public as you did twice these last few days. What you are doing is making it easier for Celestial angels to come closer to individuals on earth, not only in your city of Prescott, but elsewhere too. Yes, as someone wrote to you, people are following your journey with great interest. I too am following your life closely. I am in no rush to see you come here, but it will be a joyful day for me to greet you in person.

Blessings to you, my son; I love you with heavenly love.

For a short time, your father on earth –

Andrew.

## Jesus: *"Confirms other writers"*

I am here, your friend, Jesus –

Yes, I truly am the one that I say I am.

I am here only to confirm the writers who have come to you. You are smiling and this is good, for Hugh Taggart did write. He came because he loves you. This affection for you started when you showed such interest in him as you first read his story in the messages recorded by James Padgett. You had such a personal interest in him that you included his story in each and every book you have written and published relating to the Padgett Messages. He recognizes this and is appreciative.

I am also happy that your own father came to write again. Your soul progression will be helped a great deal by his presence and communications. He is a bright spirit loved by many.

Lastly, we are very pleased that Martin Luther continues his rapport with you. In the days ahead, he will have many interesting messages to write. He has taken a special interest in you because you responded so positively to the messages he wrote through James Padgett. There are others present who will write; for they also took notice of your attention to their writings received by James Padgett … and this includes me.

Be encouraged, Joseph. The work that you are doing is helping to create many blessings to numbers of people.

I bless you as does our Heavenly Father.

Your brother and friend – Jesus.

# PART TWO

MESSAGES FROM FAMILY

CHAPTER FOUR
# LETTERS FROM MY FAMILY

**Wednesday – December 10th, 2014**

*Morning prayers began early. I went to prayer feeling troubled. Prayers ended with several repetitions of these words from the Prayer that Jesus gave to James Padgett:*

"We pray thus with all the earnestness and longings of our souls, and trusting in Thy Love, give Thee all the glory and honor and love that our finite souls can give."

**Trust:** *Am I truly trusting in the Divine Love?*
*Am I trusting the presence of loving spirits?*
*Do I trust the Messages I have received as actually coming from the names and persons stated in the messages?*
*Do I trust I am being guided by Divine angels?*

**Mother: "*You are troubled about many things*"**

My dear son, Joseph, I am Julia, your mother –
I know that you are in doubt; I am also aware that you are in need of our presence – your Divine angel friends. Yes, I am truly your mother, though I am not in the position to prove this to you. Accept this in faith and let us see if we are able to communicate: me to write, and you to receive.

This is not the time to tell you my story and how I became

a Celestial spirit. I will do this, but not now. You are troubled about many things. You worry too much, and this disturbs your prayer and longings for the Father's Love. We are present to help, and you sense that you are not trusting. This is precisely why you repeated again and again the end of the Prayer.

And now you are surprised with my writing. I am here to help you, and you notice that it is not you doing the actual writing.

Yes, smile, for this shows you are beginning to relax. I come to comfort you with a mother's love: this I often did when you were a child filled with so many fears. I am grateful I can do this now, but in a much different way, for I see that you are in much need of comfort.

Your life is changing rapidly, even more now than in the past. You are laughing! Good! Yes, you have experienced change in the past. If I may say it this way, the changes were more stretched out; now the changes are happening in quick succession. You are in new territory.

You are wondering if you are able to do the things that appear to be opening for you to do. Remember what others have advised: Relax; and do not rush ahead with an over active imagination. Take what comes, one day at a time.

We cannot force others to respond positively to you. It does appear that doors may open for you. Is this happening too quickly?

A letter you received was a big surprise. The writer is pondering the words you spoke at the meeting at the library that you attended. You must realize that this is all new to her. If you receive an invitation to speak at her church, by all means go. Do not worry; you will do well.

Your father told you how it was for him to change and become a Celestial spirit. I am happy for him. My change came much quicker. I will tell you all about this when we have the opportunity. Yes, I know that your sister, Marie, is anxious to hear from me.

However, you are our immediate focus. We want to assist you through the next several days and, if need be, the next several months. It is a very important time in your personal life, and we add this: it is a very important time on earth for the advancement and growth of the Divine Love.

I ask you, my son, do you now feel less troubled since I have come to write? Keep up with your prayers, especially now during this time of transition.

You must do your part; no other person or Celestial spirit can do this for you. You must be more sincere and active in your prayers. Divine Love is flowing and doing what it is intended to do, namely, to change the substance of your soul into the Divine Essence.

Do not stop this process; increase your efforts. This is what we mean when we tell you to do your part. We are here and will help, but it is you that must do the work of praying and longing sincerely for the Divine Love. In no other way will the change take place.

We shall continue to assist you through our encouragements and help you to feel our love, but it is truly you, my dear son, that must cooperate and engage your efforts to receive more of the Love that comes from our Heavenly Father.

You are growing weak. Break now from writing. Go to help your family get ready for the day: your wife to teach her young students, and, you, to drive sweet Julia Rose to her school.

### Later the same day …

*Mother, if the one writing is in fact my mother, your voice does not match in my mind the person I remember as my mother from forty-five years ago.*

Now I am the one that is smiling, Joseph, for your observation is correct. I am certainly no longer the person that you have in your memory. Some of the qualities of my personality remain, but I am surely changed. When you pass over and we meet, for an instant you will not recognize me. And then what will happen is that I will come into focus, and you will know the real me.

You will be different to me also, but not as much as I will be different to you. We will make ourselves known to each other. You will know me as I am, and I will know you. It will be a happy time for you and me and, of course, for all who will be present to greet you in your new home.

As I close this message, I want to tell you that none of us here can nor do we seek to control the outcome of your conversations with other people. Be patient and trust the process. Trust us, your Celestial friends. Above all, trust the Love of our Heavenly Father. On this you can depend. The Divine Love is first and last and remains forever.

I will close now. We will write again. I comfort you with a mother's love, and I bless you.

Go now in quietness, with full assurance of our love.

I am your own mother – Julia.

## Wednesday – December 17th, 2014

*Today I begin by moving my pencil on the surface of paper, thinking by doing this I may be in the proper condition to receive a message from spirit.*

*I cannot identify the particular spirit that is present. Perhaps this will be a skill I will develop. I hope someone from my biological family is present; I would like to receive a message from anyone – my father or mother, perhaps my brother Charles or someone else.*

*Am I open enough and in condition to receive a message?*

*I wait and listen ...*

## Julia: *"A very short note"*

Yes, Joseph, I am here, your mother –

I realize how much you long to hear from us and from Charles in particular. This will take place, but before that, I would like to write a short note and it is this – be assured that we are visiting with your new friend. If you do not receive an invitation to speak at their gathering, do not be disappointed. It is not you that they will be rejecting. Please do not take it personally. Other doors of opportunity will open.

You are tired, my son, go rest and we will resume later.

## Saturday – December 27th, 2014

*This morning I woke with a desire to write – to receive a communication from spirit. I feel spirits present who may wish to write.*

*Family members that have passed have been in my thoughts. There are many now living the spirit life, and I have a feeling several of them would like an opportunity to write. Most prominent in my thought is a sister I never met; this sister died a short time after being born. Her name is Ana; she would be 90 years-old today. This is a good number of years to develop and progress in the spirit-world. Many people are unaware of this fact – a baby grows to maturity after passing. Does she desire to write and tell her story?*

## Julia: *"Knowledge of the Divine Love"*

Yes, Joseph, I am here your mother –

I am aware of your questions and interest in your family.

You ask: *Who is it that presented the awareness of the Divine Love to us, your mother and father and others?*

You sense that this person is Ana, our daughter who died, oh, so young.. You are correct; it was, indeed, Ana.

Ana was raised by loving and beautiful spirits; this is quite common in cases where children pass as infants. These loving spirits cared for her as though she was their own child. Ana and I visited often, though I was not aware of this and did not remember our visits.

As you know from your readings about these things, during a person's sleep time, there is a continuing connection with individuals, in many cases, with loved ones that have passed to the afterlife. I visited often with Ana but, as I said, did not recall these visits while I was alive in my physical body.

When I passed I awoke in my new life and was greeted by family. Ana was present and we immediately embraced, for then I remembered. We were not strangers to each other. She became my guide and teacher. She helped me to remember. I did recall this and we were reunited.

Ana had already helped your father when he passed nearly

20 years before me. As Marie has informed you, Andrew was quite psychic. He embraced what Ana and other spirits told him about the Divine Love.

Although he had received Divine Love, due to beliefs he held as a Christian minister, he had difficulty releasing the errors of belief, and so did not advance as quickly as I did. His progress was slow, much slower than mine. Yes, he is a Celestial spirit now.

Though I was late in arriving in spirit, I actually progressed into the Celestial Heaven before Andrew.

No, we are not soulmates; we are, however, close friends.

Our daughter Ana, of course, was already a Celestial angel before either Andrew or I passed. She was also present when Charles passed and helped him to adjust to his new life in spirit.

Ana is a very bright spirit, and her home is very high in the Celestial Heaven. If I may say, she is somewhat like an overseer for our family. She helps each one to accept and adjust to their new life here. Yes, Ana desires to come and write you a message. My feeling is that she and you will have a special relationship. She will speak with you about this.

This message will be very helpful to your sisters, Marie and Dorothy. Dorothy will have a more difficult time accepting this.

Marie, like yourself and your father, is receptive to influences from those in the spirit-world. Please share this message with both of them. We will be there when they read our words.

Your other sister, Margie, is very happy. She loves you a great deal and says that the books that you gave to her to read prior to her death were very helpful in preparing her for life here.

Your brother, Andy (Bundy), is doing well also; he is progressing rapidly. He is now has his home in the place above the first sphere. Ted has his home in a beautiful place in Summerland, as do your other brothers, Elmer and Bill, though not quite so high as Ted or Bundy. Bill is still too heavily attached to many of the beliefs he held when on earth. He is happy and sees no need for the Divine Love – but this will eventually change.

Your brother, Ed, is resting still. He is not yet fully awake. Eleanor, however, is awake and very happy, busy exploring her new surroundings like a little child.

Ana is so good with each family member. Her light and levity truly helps ease the transition for each person. After this, of course, it is up to each one, individually, to allow the progress of their soul. Some are open to the great change, some not so much as others.

For some reason, Elmer and Bill are not so willing to accept that Ana is really their sister. Eleanor immediately accepted her; surprisingly, Bundy and Ted also did, as did Margie. When Ed wakes completely, we feel that he will immediate recognize and accept Ana as his sister.

Joseph, I ask you to give this message time; read it often and mediate on it. I am your mother writing, with quite a bit of help from your sister, Ana. We love you very much. We desire that you be happy and at peace with yourself and the writing that you do. Do not doubt that it is you mother who writes.

I am Julia your mother, with Ana, your sister.

**Comment**

The above message from mother is pivotal. The silence between me and my family now living in the afterlife weakened when my father came to write. It was broken when my mother came to write. However, when I received news of my sister, Ana, the silence between us was almost completely shattered.

I followed through with mother's suggestion to show this message to my sisters, Marie and Dorothy.

Marie was completely receptive and happy about this. Dorothy was opposite: she liked it because it was about her family. But she made it clear that she is not open to the subject of humans communicating with spirits. I told her to think of this as an interesting story I dreamed up, because I miss them all so much.

## FAMILY INFORMATION

While living on earth Julia (mother) and Andrew (father) were married in the year 1915 and had 12 children.

**Family Names**

Many of my siblings are known to each other with a name different than their birth name. It is important to note that the "family names" are used in this book rather than only the given name to each at birth:

> Elmer
> William = Bill
> Eleanor
> Edmond = Ed
> Julia = Ana
> Charles = Charles or Charlie
> Marie
> Theodore = Ted
> Andrew = Bundy
> Margaret = Margie
> Dorothy
> Joseph (me) = Joey, Joe and Joseph

## FAMILT REUNION IN 1942 AT
## OUR FAMILY HOME IN BUFFALO, NEW YORK.

Back: Charles, Eleanor, Mom, Dad, Elmer, Marie, Ed, Bill.
Front (L to R): Margie, Joey, Dorothy, Bundy and Ted.

## Early Tuesday Morning – December 30th, 2014

*I woke early. I tried to return to sleep but was too excited and wanted to receive more of the unfolding story of my birth family now living the spirit life.*

*This story was not planned by me. Instead, it began as a huge surprise. In the beginning I resisted. When my dad first came to write I would not permit it. Then I quickly mellowed. And when my mother wrote a message I did not believe.*

*Remembering the various messages that James Padgett received from his family helped me to accept what was happening.*

*Now I am different. I am anxious to hear again from my family and to receive a message from the sister I never met and my brother Charles who died during World War II.*

*So, I am awake early today. After a brief prayer, I ask: Am I in a proper condition to receive a message? I wait ...*

## Martin Luther: *"Communications from your family"*

This is your friend Martin –

I come to write only a short note, as I realize your desire to hear from your family. The communications with them are very important, not just for you personally, but also for others who will be reading these messages.

A close connection exists between the human on earth and his or her family that have already passed into the afterlife. No one on earth is alone and separate from those no longer physically present, whether immediate family or ancestors never met.

Yes, it is true that you are each individuals; nonetheless, no one stands alone. Your individuality is shaped in the context of a human family, whether small or large. The family reaches beyond your biological roots; it extends to your community, village, city, and nation, and to the culture and the context of the specific time in human history.

So, it is with appreciation that you, Joseph, are open to experiencing contact through communications with your family living in various spirit realms.

I remain your guide and helper along with others not yet revealed to you. You are seeing the dynamics of your life on earth in relation to the ongoing life of your family in the spirit-world. Many spirits have an interest in your life and the progress of your soul; these include family and individuals such as me.

What is the aim and goal? The continuing progress of your soul is our primary purpose. This is not the only thing. Through you (and a host of others living on earth), increasing numbers will come to realize the Heavenly Father's love toward and for all His children.

Enjoy your experience as it unfolds!

I bless you as does our Heavenly Father.

Your friend and brother,

Martin – Martin Luther.

### Andrew: *"A Confirmation"*

I am here, your father –

I want to add only a word of confirmation regarding the message from Martin, that it is truly Martin Luther who writes to you, and that he is one of your special guides. I also want to say that it was your mother who wrote you the message a few days ago.

It surprises you that she writes so well and so beautifully. If you could see her, this would be an even greater surprise. She is a radiant person, very beautiful indeed. Her beauty and the ability to write messages to you is evidence of the great change that the Divine Love has made in her soul.

We are aware that you wish to hear more about how this happened in our lives. The story continues and it is indeed a wonderful love story to be told and shared. But I will close for now and allow another of your family to come and write.

Bless you, my son. I love you, as I love all your brothers and sisters.

Peace and love be with you, and blessings from our Heavenly Father – Andrew, your dad.

**Continued – December 30th, 2014**

**Ana:** *"My experience and family information"*

My dearest brother, Joseph, I am your sister Ana –

Yes, I see that you are surprised and happy, and that you have tears in your eyes. The tears we have are of happiness and joy.

I wanted to write "Joey" but refrained. Though I did not have the pleasure and joy of meeting you on earth, I want to say that I was always nearby, not just when you were born, but at the birth and lives of all the younger ones in the family – Dorothy and Margie, and the boys, Bundy and Ted. But you were the last born and so of special interest to me. You were born during a very difficult time in the family. And in your nation, there was a beginning of war. I say this so you that you may know of the care and guidance that surrounds each child of the Father in human life. We, the angels in spirit, are the Father's helpers.

When you were young I was developing rapidly. In your earth measurement of time I was not yet eleven years-old. My care-givers and teachers here were kind and very gentle, leading us to the awareness of the Father's Love, but never forceful and demanding. I was a happy child and explored everything around us without fear. We were safe in our environment. I learned quickly. We do not have the impediments and hindrances that you do in your earth life. As our mother informed you, she and I had a continuing connection after I passed as a baby. She visited regularly, even when I was but an infant. So, from the beginning of my growth from a baby to the development of my self-awareness, with the help of the nurse-maids and teachers I learned that I was a child of a very large earth family. I was introduced to know each one of you, as well as my own location in the family. I grew to become more aware of each of you than any of you were of me.

By the time members of the family began to arrive in the spirit-world, I had advanced in my development to the first

Celestial Heaven. I was young according to earth measurements of time – eighteen years of age.

You have been asking questions, and I will try to answer. You asked how it was that I became aware of the Divine Love. The simple and plain truth is that I was nursed and raised by individuals who know this information and experienced the Divine Love as a soul-changing ingredient freely available to all that desire it. They did not force this awareness upon me or any other child. But it was the environment of our experience. We still needed to make the choice for this Love, but the choice was really easy.

We lived and grew in this atmosphere of loving souls. I wanted to live as they lived and was instructed how this was possible. We were never taught error. Thus, as we grew we had no need to unlearn what we were taught as individuals born and raised in the earth environment must do when they arrive here. This is the grace and beauty of our Heavenly Father's Love. Our growth and development in this Great Love has few encumbrances and hindrances.

Later, as you are able to receive my messages, I will share more about how this all plays out and how we may quickly pass through the various realms of spirit to enter the Celestial Heaven. What I have shared with you today is an introduction to my life here.

Now, allow me to introduce a new subject that I know is of deep interest to you and to Marie, namely, our brother, Charles.

As you know, Charles and I were close in age. As I grew and developed in my life in spirit, Charles was experiencing his growth in a completely different environment. Yet, my guides and teachers here had me stay in touch with Charles in a closer way than the lives of my older siblings.

Looking back, it was their soul perceptions that had them do this. It was not inevitable or predetermined that Charles would be the first to arrive here as an adult. The circumstances in your world, involved as it as in continual turmoil and war, made us very aware of the sufferings of humans and their families. We were all on high alert. Though we tried very hard to guide and help people on earth, we would not interfere directly. Thus, though very sad to behold, individuals by scores began to arrive here. We were ready; we were trained in what to do to help the suffering people. When Charles arrived, we were present to help. I was present to help Charles in his transition.

Charles, along with many other soldiers, arrived here in a condition of shock and bewilderment. He felt lost and somewhat angry.

I met him soon after he arrived, but I did not identify myself as his sister. The gentleness and kindness I showed him worked wonders for a quick adjustment to his new life. I was not the only one present to help him; there were many of us, each with a slightly different task. I was one of many, helping not only Charles but other young men and women as well.

Charles was a bright and alert young man, delightful to be near. With the help of special teachers and healers, he quickly realized that he did not carry his physical body into the spirit life. He recognized that he was not alone but in a new and safe environment. We worked with him – as we worked with all others – to be healed of the memories of warfare and killing and death.

At first Charles was angry and bitter, but he possessed a good heart and soul, and soon was healed and on his way to full recovery and prepared for his new life here. All this took place in less than a year. He was soon all smiles, laughter and questions, and inquisitiveness. He progressed and, now, some 70 years later, he lives in a beautiful home in the Celestial Heaven.

When I first revealed my identity to Charles he was silent. He did not believe babies that died young actually live and grow. But when I described my life here and my continuing relationship with mother, his skepticism disappeared and we became very close friends. Now we often work as a team when someone from our family passes and arrives here.

Charles will come soon and tell you his own story. I think what I have written is a good introduction. You and I have much yet to talk about. This is already a long message.

I feel happy to be able to communicate in this way with you. You are receiving our thoughts very accurately. As we proceed we will share many other interesting things about our experiences in the spirit-world.

Help yourself daily, Joseph. We can come to encourage and teach you, but it will be you that must make the effort to progress with the Divine Love within you.

Yes, in answer to your question: I do know my soulmate; we have joined in the beautiful reunion of our origin. I hope to tell you about this in a future message.

We will write again soon.

I love you and bless you as does our Heavenly Father.

Go in peace and with our love,

Your loving sister and friend – Ana.

## Comment

The above message from my sister in the afterlife is another pivotal "breaking the silence" moment. Every time I read it, I'm carried to a place of awe.

I may never tire of the realization that I am actually reading a letter from a sister that I never met. The afterlife is – as many others have before stated – a land of many surprises.

## Sunday – January 4th, 2015

*Five days later: It has not been as easy as I assumed it would be to maintain an openness, willingness and desire to continue to receive communications from spirit. For one thing I have been lazy, also more interested in activities with my family during the holidays. This morning I woke early with an inclination to go to my office to write, but I chose to linger in bed and finally fell asleep and woke much later than usual.*

*So, I am here after a very nice session in prayer.*

## Ana: *"Each moment is new"*

I am here, your sister, Ana –

Please write as I guide you.

You are not as far from us as you feel that you are. We are near and we love you. Your prayer was very effective and meaningful for those here that listened and participated. Your words go quickly to the Father as sincere longings of your soul and He answered with a good amount of the Divine Love.

You are correct in saying that you are beginning a new day, and that you have never been here before. It is a new place where you now stand. Each moment is new; it is a gradual ascent to higher places. Be assured that we have not abandoned you. We remain by your side. Go forth in peace and joy.

Others are waiting to write. Yes, your brother Charles is present. We feel you are somewhat hesitant. This is understandable. Your present experience is part of the newness you feel. Breathe deeply. Do not worry whether you are in proper condition. We are ready. We would not tell you this if we saw that you are not ready. Do not close yourself to this new experience. Charles is sweet and gentle, just as you have experienced the same about mother and father and me. You have also experienced the same qualities of kindness and helpfulness in the presence of Martin and other spirit friends. Go now and prepare yourself.

Your loving sister – Ana.

*I pause. I am breathing deeply and slowly. I am experiencing difficulty accepting the possibility of the presence of my beloved brother, Charles. This is hard for me to comprehend and accept. I last saw and spoke with Charles when I was a nine-year-old boy. He was my idol and hero. Now, I am an old man and excited. I feel I am now ready. I feel like a young child and want to run and jump into his arms!*

## Charles: *"My experience in passing"*

Hello Joseph! This is strange; I intended to write "Joey" but the name "Joseph" was written instead.

I am laughing, for I am excited too. It has been many years since we last talked – me as your older brother, and you, a small kid of nine. And here you are now, an older man wearing a grey beard. How different! If you could see me, I would stand before you with the appearance of a young man, perhaps 32 years-old or so.

Yes, it is true; I am your brother, Charles, and I do live in the Celestial Heaven.

When on earth I knew nothing of this, and when I arrived here – I mean in spirit – I knew next to nothing. The memories of my few short years on earth have nearly faded. It would be like you trying to recall details from your life as a child. So, I am thankful you are not waiting with a barrel full of questions. Some I might be able to answer but perhaps not all.

Our dear sister, Ana -- Oh, what a surprise it was when she came to me after I arrived in this spirit-world! How could I have possibly known that she would be here?

I do not recall knowing that I had a sister that died shortly after birth. I do not recall that anyone in our family ever spoke to me about a sister that died before I was born. This is one thing I do not remember. Our sister, Dorothy, probably represents a true picture of our knowledge about this: Dorothy tried to correct you when she heard you say that there were twelve in our family. We were not taught to remember Ana. Thus, I came here with the awareness of eleven children – not twelve. So, after I died in the war, I arrived here with incomplete awareness about our family.

As far as my death and transition, it was difficult. War is a horrible and an unnatural thing. This is true no matter which side you are on. However, the thoughts of the mind were much worse than the experience of death. The pain of the body was little compared to the lingering, ignorant thoughts and images conjured up by the mind. I was scared, not fully knowing what was happening to me.

Thankfully, I died quickly, and when I arrived here I thought I was hallucinating. One moment I am on a bed of blood, and the next moment I am in a place of calmness, of beauty and rest. There were many loving people visiting all the soldiers arriving from battles.

One very beautiful girl stood out among all the others that came to us to help and assist us. She was more beautiful to me than any other lovely female that I had ever seen. Of course, I did not know who she was or even where I was. And this is why I thought that I was dreaming. I had no reference point. I was ignorant.

This young girl came to me often, and I liked her presence. She seemed to me to be about my own age. Yes, she visited others, but she appeared to take a special interest in me. We talked often, but I am sure it was one-sided, where she did most of the talking.

She helped me to realize that I had died in the war. I remember feeling strange. She helped me see that my physical body was gone and that I had a different kind of body – a body that was similar and the same shape, but of a different density. She taught me that this is my spirit-body, and that it had been with me all along while on earth, and that my physical body was like a temporary covering for my spirit-body.

She also taught me that I was now living in a different world, a different dimension – a different life. For some reason I found this easy to accept. For instance, I discovered that I was able to walk and run and jump. When I hit the ground, I did not suffer pain. I did not get winded when I ran.

The world I found myself in is a beautiful place; it has trees and flowers and streams. All I could think about this was how beautiful and peaceful it is here. I began to love where I was and did not make an attempt – as many others did – to return to earth. I felt that I belonged here – that this was my real home, and where I was meant to be.

Well, the girl I began to tell you about was an excellent teacher. She knew so much about this world. She helped me to realize that I was not dead, not really – but that I was now fully alive – more alive than ever.

Well, one day, when we were talking about our life in this world, and our family still on earth, she said that my mother had another child, born just one year before I was born. I was curious about this and to help me understand, she showed me records of our family.

Yes, there really are records of this kind here. You have already read about this fact in other books available to you on earth, yet I see that you are a bit surprised that I write about these records. But you need to realize that I did not know this. I also discovered that they have fantastic libraries here. You can read and study as much as you choose.

So, after this research, other teachers informed me that the girl I admired so much is my sister – my sister, Ana. I grew silent when her identity was revealed to me. How could this be? I asked my teachers: How does an infant grow in this world? This was too good to be true! Then something quickly happened. I felt that some sort of cord went from me to her – not a literal cord – but a cord of connection. The news that she is my sister established a bond. The news felt right; it felt true.

I hugged her. We held each other in this embrace for a long time. After this experience I could not tolerate to be away from her. I stayed as close as possible to her. I listened closely to her words and she taught me even more and greater things. Because of her I am here today writing this message to you – my kid brother.

Oh, Joseph, I have so much more to write and tell you. I am a thankful person to be able to come and write and tell you my story. In the days to come, I, along with mom and dad and Ana, and many other friends in this life, wish to tell people on earth what it is *really* like to live in this world.

I realize that you have many books on this subject on earth, but what we write will bring added and fresh perspectives that humans will enjoy reading. The books you have in your world cannot possibly contain all that can be written about our life in the spirit-world.

I have only started, and I am looking forward to coming to you again to continue our story. I hope that you have enjoyed this experience today. Thank you, Joey! Thank you, Joseph!

I love you; we all love you.

Peace and love from your family and all your spirit friends,

I am your brother – Charles.

## Thursday – January 8th, 2015

*I remain in awe of the communications that I am receiving from my family in the spirit-world. I entertain the thought that I must remain open, and that I make no conscious effort to interfere or attempt in any way to impose my will on what shall or shall not be written. It is a fantastic story and I have the feeling that it is just the beginning.*

*A question lingers: Since my sister, Ana, has been revealed as the influence to bring awareness of Divine Love to my mother and dad, and to Charles, has Ana had a similar influence in my life?*

*In addition, is Martin Luther now stepping aside as the primary guide in these writings? Is there some other guide leading the orchestration of the writers that come to me to write? I suppose I am really asking this: Where do I go from here? I feel that I am still standing at an open door and everything is new!*

### Mathew (Apostle): *"Remain a willing student"*

Joseph, my friend, I am Matthew –

I have not written you before, but I have been near and have seen your family appear. Yes, I am confirming that you have received messages from your own mother, father, a sister and one brother. Each is indeed the true person they represent themselves to be. You are moving past doubt of this; I thought my additional confirmation will further help to you.

In one sense your position is similar to the experience of James Padgett. Do not be alarmed that I say this. No; we are not suggesting something as ambitious as what we did with James. He is first, the forerunner of others. We are not moving in the direction of giving you new revelations as we did with him. I mention him to describe the similar feelings you have as the result of receiving messages from your family.

You are asking important questions: Where is this going? Who is my guide? Why am I receiving this information? What am I to do with it?

I suggest that you remain open. Be a willing student. Hold fast to your knowledge of the Divine Love and remain steadfast in prayer. What you are experiencing directly results from your years of praying and longing for the Father's Love. Your transformation continues and will continue as long as you stay the course that brought you to this point.

Yes, I am Matthew an Apostle of Jesus, our Master and elder brother. I come today to encourage you to continue.

There are others here who also are interested in what you

are doing. Be a happy disciple who loves doing the will of the Father.

I have written all that I desire to say at this time. I am pleased to introduce myself to you. We are anticipating an interesting development of the messages that you are receiving and will continue to receive. Remain open to what is taking place, and do not cease in your longings for the Divine Love.

I am your brother and friend – Matthew.

## Martin Luther: *"Many spirits assist you"*

This is Martin here, yes, Martin Luther –

I am here to answer your question: was it your sister, Ana that led you to the awareness of the Divine Love? The answer is both yes and no.

There is not just one spirit-friend working alone who assisted you to discover the messages of truth concerning the Divine Love in the writings of James Padgett. There were and are many spirits used by the Father to bring this news to you. Many seeds were planted during your life: stepping stones leading you to the path you chose to take.

No spirit forced you in the direction that you walked. Many spirits were present at times in influencing you; but, no spirit coerced you or brought over-bearing influence. This is not our way. We always maintain a delicate balance of your will and desire and the presence of our influence.

Imagine a chorus of spirits singing beautiful melodies. The voice of the chorus is not loud and boisterous, commanding attention. No; it is a light sound – barely audible. It requires that the human be in sufficient silence to hear the melodies that are being sung. A small portion of the music heard here, another there – and longer experiences at a particular place – all leading to the complete song of the presence of love where the human soul may be enraptured in this experience.

Your family has been present in different and varying degrees of influence. Yes, Ana, your sister remains an active guide in your life. Your father is also an important presence in your life. Because of his theological training his influence has been very helpful in the different aspects of your journey. Your mother has also been present; her influence has been and remains a solid foundation of gentleness and kindness: and likewise, with your brother, Charles.

This is not all. There are many other spirits who have assisted you along the way. We are all happy to be a close and active part in your development and progress.

Let me now speak about the open door you sense near.

We desire that you not feel overwhelmed by all that is presently unfolding before you. It is good to take breaks and pause from this work. You are being changed by the messages received from your family; you require rest in order to assimilate the information. You are approaching deeper levels in the expansion of your soul. Your soul desires to expand as the result of the contact with Celestial friends and family. This expansion cannot proceed too rapidly. Your mortal existence in physicality prohibits instantaneous change.

You are correct in saying that you must not attempt to impose an overall story to the messages that you receive. Allow the writers to speak their own individual voice. Do not make them fit into your world of understanding. Relax and be patient; the story will emerge. The better you are able to relax and be patient the better will be the reception and content of the messages.

Remember, you have only been receiving these messages for a very short time. In addition, we know you need to give time to your family and have other responsibilities.

As Matthew urged in his message, remember the foundation that brought you to this place, namely, faith and prayer. Never move away from this foundation.

I love you Joseph.

I am you brother and friend – Martin Luther.

## Andrew: *"Not an imagination of your dreams"*

I am here, your father –

It is very good that you received two very important letters, one from Matthew and the other from Martin Luther. I feel humbled and honored to be present and witness these two men writing to you. Previously I only knew of them in an intellectual way, one from my study of the Bible, and the other as part of my experiences within the Christian Church. And now, here I am a spirit, standing in their presence and witnessing these great individuals writing letters to my own son on earth. I am continually astonished with life in the spirit-world. I am, therefore, also humbled in your presence, Joseph. Yes, your own father says this about you. It is true.

I ask of you, Joseph, that you write this and keep what I wrote. Do not change it or erase it. Keep it for others to read and ponder.

What is happening here, with the spirits coming to you as they do, is not a wild imagination of your dreams. It is happening right now in the spirit-world and I cannot begin to name all those that are present and looking on.

I realize that there are many others on earth today receiving messages from the spirit-world. And now you have a unique opportunity to add a significant voice from spirits to humanity.

We will assist you every way that we can. Be strong, Joseph. Be our voice. Please, I urge you, go on with these writings. There is much to be said and shared.

I love you my son; I embrace you with a holy kiss.

Your once father on earth, a very short time – Andrew.

## Julia: *"A love for the Father's work"*

Dearest sweet Joseph –

I love you and give you a very firm hug – just the way that I used to do on earth. Do you feel it? I am so proud that you do this writing. I assure you, many will be blessed when they read the things that have been given to you.

Do not hold back. It is not pride that you have, but a love for our Heavenly Father's work. And the truth is this: All are His beloved children.

With a mother's love for her son,

I am – Julia.

## Charles: *"My kid brother"*

Hello Joey!

There, now, I was able to say *Joey* this time! You remain my kid brother! Yes, Celestial angels can speak like I am doing. Words can't express the joy I feel writing and communicating with you.

Please convey my special love to our sister, Marie. She is happy to be reading these messages, but I feel that she will enjoy seeing that I remember her and love her. When she arrives here, she will be greeted by all of us. Now I am laughing, because I want her to know we are not trying to rush her to come here.

Please take your time, Marie! We are not going anywhere. In addition, you have a lot of joy and love to spread around to your family and other people.

Thank you, Joey, for allowing me to write this note for Marie - for I realize that you are tired.

Your true brother, Charles.

## Comment

I read the letter from Charles aloud to my sister, Marie. When I did this, she laughed and cried. She and Charles were very close; Marie loved him very deeply. A college paper that she wrote to honor her brother brought high praises from the faculty. She has kept the original all these years.

## Friday – January 9th, 2015

*I am feeling that Charles, and my sister, Ana, desire to write their experiences of their life in spirit. I pray that various books I have read on the subject of life in the spirit-world will not hinder clear reception of messages from my family. I will try to be a clear channel. Continuing prayers for openness to God's beautiful Grace is the help I seek. I realize I can only do my best not to impose my limited understanding of the material that Charles and Ana wish to share with me and readers of their messages.*

*Now, with an attitude of gratefulness, I wait in silence…*

## Charles: *"More about my experience in the spirit-world"*

I am here, Charles, your brother –

I would like to continue my story. Let us experiment and see what may come now that you are in the condition to receive.

After Ana had been with me during my adjustment to life here, one day she said, "Charles, my dear brother, it is time that I leave you and return to my home. But first, I will escort you to the place where you may see your home."

What she said startled me, yet not so much that I felt fear or sadness: for I felt that I was ready to begin my own life here. She had been so kind in showing me all the various places of this new world. I realized that she would not always be with me.

Ana had her life, and I had mine, or the beginning of it. I knew that she had a home elsewhere, very far away and in a much higher place more beautiful than I had yet seen.

One day Ana took me on a journey. I mean this in a most literal sense. In fact, she *carried* me might be the better word to use: *She carried me to see her home.* Of course, I could not stay long; my condition would not permit a lengthy visit. We live in a particular location in the spirit-world because this is where our soul condition enables us to be. Her soul development was of such a high nature that she had to "tone down" her energy to be with me. And when she carried me to see her home, she had to give a portion of her "power" to me that would enable me to be with her in her location. I was not capable of staying long. Somehow, she was able to shield me; it was as though she enveloped me in a "cocoon" so that I could travel with her. I am trying to use words to help you see and understand my experience. We traveled by energies of "thought" – Ana's thoughts, not mine.

We traveled a great distance above terrain unfamiliar in beauty that I have ever seen or imagined. I have no words to describe what I saw and experienced. Her home is indescribable. Shall I even attempt? I am no poet and it would require words of a poet to attempt a word-picture of what it is that I saw. There was something about her location in a beautiful environment that caused me to be deeply uncomfortable; I could not, even with her assistance, stay long. The feeling was that I did not belong. Even her appearance changed; she was brighter, more beautiful than anyone I had ever seen. I think she gave me a brief look of what and who she really is – a Celestial angel. She turned exceptionally radiant. I could barely look into her eyes or even appreciate her smile.

Thus, after a short visit, Ana carried me again away from her home in this heavenly place. The visit was enough, however, that, as the result of this introduction, I knew with certainty that I would one day also live in a place like her home.

And so, after this experience, Ana escorted me to my new home. As we came close I felt such a peaceful feeling of belonging that I knew I was home. Everything felt right; I knew this is where I was supposed to be.

My home was located in the country, in the midst of trees and flower gardens, streams of water flowing nearby. There were small cottages, also buildings that looked like apartments, and larger buildings that looked similar to a school or college. Some homes were too large for only one person. We could be alone if we chose, or we could freely mingle with neighbors, who quickly became our friends. Some were like me, newly arrived. Others were residents that had been here a long time. And then there were the teachers and guides and advisors. I was excited to be here in my new home.

Everything was harmonious. All the buildings were constructed in such a beautiful way that made everything feel open and inviting – inviting our curiosities and inquisitiveness. I felt ready to learn and explore. I felt very much at home here, and very safe.

So, when the time came to say goodbye to Ana, I was ready. I felt certain that it was not a final parting, for I knew she would come often to visit with me. I quickly learned that when I thought of her in a certain way, she would soon thereafter appear, and we would visit.

Before she departed I said, "Ana, I want to see your first home here, the place where you arrived as a baby, and had your growth. I want you to tell me more about this place while I am viewing your first home. Will this be possible? I would really like to do that."

Ana answered and said: "I am delighted to hear you ask this. I would love to show and talk about my first home here. I often visit there and will take you with me. This will be later, after you have had time to learn and progress here in your first home."

My brother, you have been told that I slowly and eventually progressed to the Celestial Heaven. This did not happen quickly. You might wonder why my progress was slow. The answer is simply that I enjoyed every step of my progression; I took my time. I was never lonely, and I never felt that I was alone. I loved the variety of learning experiences, and still do, even in the Celestial spheres where I now live and have my home. After all, you realize that our life here is one of wonderment and surprises.

We are not forced to be on a schedule; there are no pressures placed on us that push in one direction or another. I am fortunate that I have a wonderful sister to talk to and receive her counsel and advice. Yet, even with the knowledge she shared about her home and how to progress to that location, I took my time investigating and learning in my first home. I stayed there, according to your earth time, about two years. After this I progressed rather quickly through the various levels or planes of the Second Sphere and was in the Third Sphere when our dad died and came to this location, the spirit-world.

Ana came to tell me about dad's transition, and we went together to greet him. I will leave the telling of this story for another day.

We did very good work today – actually better than I anticipated. We are both rather new at this. Well, it is all new to me. I am thankful that you have a band of helpers and guides round about you; if you didn't, I could not write a letter such as this. It is actually very difficult to recall things from many years ago. And I feel that I am often searching for right words to use for what I wish to say.

I hope you enjoyed what we wrote today.

I love you, Joseph, both as a brother and a friend.

I now leave you with my blessings and love,

Charles.

## Comment

I have read this message many times. Each time it is a new experience. I have used these words before and I feel confident to say that I will say this again and again: *I feel in awe and very humble to be receiving these messages from my family in the afterlife.*

Is it only because I am family that I feel this way? My answer is no. In fact, the truth is that I recognize the individuality of family members who come to write: I see each one in a different light than I remember of their life on earth, and I am always learning who and what they are now in their spirit-world life.

In his message, Charles blessed me to see a small aspect of his present life. It is only a brief glimpse. How is it possible for him to give a complete picture of who he is and becoming? I sensed his struggle to recall memories of his early days in spirit, or even to recall memories of his life on earth.

Add to this is the realization that I am at the beginning of my ability to receive messages from the afterlife.

CHAPTER FIVE
# THE STORY OF DAD'S DEATH

**Monday – January 19th, 2015**

*Today feels like another one of those "open door days"—where I feel that I have not been this way before. There is another new door waiting for me to walk through. What is on the other side? What and who is waiting? As I write these words I realize that the door is open and I am already lifting one foot over the threshold. Who is here, waiting and ready to write a new message?*

*I have experienced quite a variety of thoughts and feelings since writing ten days ago. Some, it seems to me, have been short visualizations of life on the other side of the veil. Others have been about me, here and now, wrestling with the familiar feelings where I waver and feel incompetent to receive what spirits desire to show and write.*

*If it is only me and a story I am creating, I can handle the criticism that I may receive. But when it comes down to it – this is not really about me. I am involved in writing the story of other people, persons no longer living on the earth. I ask: Am I getting their words correctly? Having said this, now, as best as I am able, I relax and wait...*

**Charles: *"Assisting father when he passed"***

We are both here, Joseph – your brother and sister. I am

here, Ana. And I am here, Charles, and I will be the first to write.

I have heard your questions: you have asked about my progression and development.

In my previous letter I spoke of my slow progress and said I did this because I enjoyed the experience of investigation and learning. This is true. It is also true that I could not progress beyond my actual condition.

When I did advance to higher planes and spheres, something momentous happened that caused the acceleration of my desire to proceed with my development. Please remember that the presence of Ana and her greater light and love, was a constant reminder to me of the great change available and waiting. Not everyone here has the knowledge and will to change and develop the soul with the Divine Love. Ana gave me the gift of this knowledge, but it was up to me to grasp it as an ideal for me personally.

Up until this time, I was more interested in the development of my interests of the mind and what could be learned of the life of the new world that I was experiencing. But then I had what some will call a "soul awakening." What is this? How did this happen to me? What brought it about? I will tell you.

One day Ana came to me and said that it was time to visit earth with her. She asked that I go with her to earth to visit family. When we began our journey, she prepared me with the purpose for our visit, and where we were going. She told me that our dad was dying, and that we were going to the other side, to earth, in order to be with him and assist in his transition.

At first it was difficult for me to accept what Ana was telling me. I had not done this before – well, not exactly – for I did assist to some degree the transition of soldiers when they died in battle. I did this during the time I was being healed of my involvement with the Great War. I assisted American soldiers; but mainly, I worked with Germans. But going with Ana was so much different. We were going in order to be with dad.

Ana, of course, did not know dad intimately on a physical basis as I did. Memories of my life on earth flooded my soul. What would it be like for me to actually see dad again? I did not anticipate I would have the kind of feelings that I had.

I was a bit on edge. After all, this was my own family that I was in journey with Ana to see. I hadn't seen family in years – except for a brief visit soon after I died in order to see Marie and console her. This was different; I was going with Ana to be with dad and help in his transition.

Ana assured me that the family would not see us; there would be no recognition of our presence. She informed me that dad's physical condition would be much different than any memory I might have of him. And he would be mostly asleep. Mother would be present, I was told, and our sister, Margie, nearby. No one else would be present. Our task, Ana said, would be to carry dad, his spirit body, to the Home of Rest.

When we arrived at our destination, I recognized the place: it was the home where I lived before I went off to the army. I knew the room well. It was the bedroom of my mom and dad. I wanted to visit the rest of our home and inspect each and every room, but I did not do this. We were here for a specific purpose; a solemn moment.

Mother was in the room attending to her husband. She had aged since I last saw her. And dad, well, he was lying in bed, so little and frail that I hardly recognized him. We entered the room unnoticed. Ana went directly to mom and kissed her cheek. A tear fell from mom's eye. I followed her example and kissed her other cheek, and whispered "I love you, mom." I also went to Margie and hugged her, and whispered, "I love you, Margie." She shuttered when I did this; she felt something. Ana and I stood close to the bed and looked on dad. He was ready. We saw his spirit body rise. I reached for his hand and lifted him into my arms. Ana again kissed mother: we departed, carrying dad to his waiting bed in the Home of Rest.

Dad slept in my arms during our return journey. Ana led the way. Our initial work was completed. When we arrived, the healers were waiting. Dad was placed on a bed. He was in a good place; a healing environment. The air is fresh and clean; the fragrance of flowers everywhere; the room bright and restful – a perfect place for dad to awake to his new life in spirit.

Ana and I departed but did not go far. We walked slowly to the garden and sat on the velvet green carpet of grass near the pond of refreshing water. We sat close together; we were silent, not with sadness, but with happy anticipation that we were together to assist dad in his transition to new life.

Here, I began to realize the awakening of my soul. Ana read my thoughts. We communicated on a deep level of our soul. Until this time I had not experienced the soul on this level. I realized that this was the beginning of a new phase in my life in spirit. One might say that this is the moment I became more serious about my future.

Why do I say this? I saw clearly the responsibility that Ana assumed when I died in the war and made my entrance to life here. She was present for me, and now, together, we are present for our dad. What we will do and say shall make a tremendous difference in our dad's healing process.

I saw that this experience as the beginning: there would be the arrivals of other family members. If we will not be present, who would be here to greet them and assist the adjustment to new life in the spirit? I leaned over and kissed Ana on the cheek, smiled and said, "I love you Ana; thank you."

When dad arrived here he was not in good condition. His spirit body was nearly the appearance of his frail physical body. By comparison, my own beginning here was completely different. I was young, and except for the experiences in combat I was in excellent physical condition. Dad arrived looking very much like an old man; as the result of the cancer in his body his physical condition was one of skin and bones. He also came here with a baggage of emotional scars. His recovery was certain and yet slowed by deep wounds. But because of our presence, Ana's in particular, we saw his recovery advance in remarkable ways. The work of the healers wrought beautiful results.

Many humans arrive here without intimate connection with loving family. Healing is blocked to a degree where the love connection to family does not exist; for some individuals healing does not happen for a very long time. I've been shown persons in this condition and it is not a scene I care to see again. When I arrived having Ana's presence helped to change my condition quickly. I responded to her care and love. But I have already shared with you that part of my story.

We were still sitting in the garden near the pond. I sighed, and Ana reached her soft hand to mine. She understood my thoughts and feelings. We looked deeply into each other's eyes and smiled. We agreed that our love would indeed help our dad recover.

I knew that he would be well and happy.

### Ana: *"Progress and development"*

I am here, Ana, your sister –

Charles has given you a wonderful description of our dad's arrival here.

Now you are asking many questions about laws of compensation and the process of expiation. If your questions persist, I suggest that you ask these questions of Martin and others. My observation is that your questions will disappear as you continue to receive our messages.

I have already written you about my experience. A child, especially an infant, has few or no injuries in her precious soul.

What small amount of flaw there is exists as the result of absorbing the condition of the parents. It does not belong to the child and quickly disappears in the loving environment in which they are cared for.

Love works amazing things in our life here. This is particularly true when the Divine Love is present in the lives of the care-givers and healers on little children. Love – the Divine Love – is of such a nature that precious little children feel and readily respond to it. So, yes, there is some residue in a child's soul. It is addressed quickly and easily in our homes for children. It is not a complicated matter, but rather simple.

In your readings of this subject in various books about life here in the spirit-world, in messages to humans from spirits, especially in the foundation messages received by James Padgett, you have learned that humans, soon after they arrive in this world of spirit, settle in a location fitting the condition of their soul. Some may remain in a certain location for many years until such time as they have an awakening and progress to a different and higher place. This you know as the Law of Progress.

The various locations are not places of torment and punishment created by our loving Heavenly Father. Instead, these locations may be understood as homes of rescue and healing, and no person is ever held in these places against their will. They may leave and go to a better place any time they choose and desire to change.

As you have recited many times from the prayer that Jesus gave to humanity, *"only we ourselves can prevent love making the great change in our life."* Love is always waiting for the person to make the change and progress to a higher and more beautiful and happier place.

For example, you have read the stories told to James Padgett of the progress of such souls as Julius Caesar and Nero, and how they suffered for hundreds of years and, yet, when they finally opened to the possibility of change and progress, they responded, and change for them happened rather rapidly. There are examples of thousands upon thousands of people who have similar stories; their stories remain untold and unknown. God's Great Love has no limits, for it extends to each and all people everywhere.

We showed you only a glimpse of Charles' life here, but we have not told you each and every detail of his development. Again, the process is not complicated, but very simple. Life in the spirit-world is open and clearly visible, and help is everywhere to be seen and experienced. From the smallest blade of grass, to the beautiful range of flowers and trees and landscape: everything tells the glory and benefit of love and harmony.

We learn just by being here in such a lovely and pure environment of love. When you consider the presence of teachers everywhere, the opportunities for growth and progress abound. Charles was, and still is, a very happy learner. Nonetheless, he is the one who will make choices along the way that will determine the progress and development with the Divine Love.

He has told you that he made a decision at the death and passing of our dad. He said it was a moment of his soul awakening. After that, the rate of his progress increased by leaps and bounds, and he soon experienced the great change and entered into the greater happiness found in the Celestial world.

We will come again and tell you more about the arrival of Andrew, our dad, and how he experienced the joy of awaking to his new life in spirit.

With all my love, and the love and blessings from our Heavenly Father,

I am your sister – Ana.

## Saturday – January 24th, 2015

*Early this morning I reviewed messages beginning with one received from Jesus on Saturday, November 29th, 2014. I did this because I had an interest to read again what I have receive from the afterlife. After I finished the message of Jesus I felt inspired to go on and read what followed.*

*I believe this review helped me to see the value in the writings I have been receiving from the spirit-world. I do not write without pause to consider the content of the material being received. I was surprised to read again how often I had received encouragement to continue with these writings. In fact, I read again a message from my dad, where he asked me not to erase what he wrote. I did not erase anything!*

*Today I feel that I am prepared to proceed. I am asking Charles and Ana to return and continue with their story of the experience of our dad in the Home of Rest. With their help, I now write the story ...*

## Charles and Ana: *"Dad's experience in the Home of Rest"*

After pause, Ana spoke, "It is time, Charles; dad is beginning to stir awake. We will wait for a call from the healers to return. I am being told that there will be a special person present to greet dad and welcome him to his new life. I have been instructed to ask you to do this, Charles. I will accompany you. Let us go now. We are being called."

We walked with purpose to the Home of Rest. When we arrived, the four healers located around the bed where dad was resting, sensed our presence. They smiled and waved us near. We came close and saw that the figure of the man was much different than when we carried him here from the bedroom in his home on earth.

Dad was wearing a robe of light grey with a whisper of pale green. He began to stir when Ana and I came near. It was obvious that he felt our presence. Then, in very soft tones, standing some distance away, the healers began to sing a most lovely song. Dad loved music and this was such a wonderful touch, so very pleasant to awaken to. Other individuals came and began to join the circle gathering for dad's welcome. Even with increased numbers the music remained soft and quiet. The sweet melody welcomed dad to his new life.

Dad's eyes slowly opened. He looked around; we saw that he was trying to focus on what he was experiencing. A faint smile of recognition showed on his face. Some individuals in a similar situation awake with alarm, and some, in a state of fear. Not so with dad. His eyes fully opened and he glanced at me, and his eyes grew bigger and a huge smile graced his face. To myself only, I said "I believe dad recognizes me!" Ana heard and conveyed the thought: "Yes, Charles, he knows."

"Welcome home, dad," were my first words to him. And I leaned over and kissed his cheek.

Dad threw out his arms and hugged me tightly. "I am here," he said, "I am finally here. And who but my own son is here to greet me – just as I anticipated that he would. I feel so happy to see you, and my, oh my, you look so well and strong."

"Yes, dad, I am indeed your son, Charles. We were told by others of your coming. We visited your home on earth and carried you here. Now you are safe and well. Would you like me to help you to stand?"

Dad laughed with happiness. And with only a little help from me he stood. When he did this, the visitors clapped. Gladness and joy was present in this place of rest and welcome. He beamed with gratefulness and happiness. "I am blessed," he spoke to all. "Somehow I saw something like this before I died. But I did not dream that death could be such a wonderful experience like this. So, it is true? Am I truly here? Or could it be that I am still dreaming?"

I laughed; many present also did. "Yes, dad, your experience is the beginning of your new life. The individuals gathered here know you. Perhaps you will not recognize each one. They have come to welcome you."

One by one they came close to dad. Many did not really need to speak their name; dad recognized them and greeted each one individually – his own mother and father, and his brother, John, and other family members, and people he once knew really well when he was their pastor on earth. It was a happy time of reunion.

After this, Ana and I were again alone with dad. Dad's time of welcome went very smoothly. In the distance we heard the people continue their song of welcome. The music filled the atmosphere with harmony and joy.

We saw that dad was visibly tired. I said to him, "It's alright dad, you may return to your bed for rest. We will stay close. Then, after you rest, if you choose, we can talk." He smiled with gratitude. He sat on the bed, and then slowly reclined and was quickly asleep.

Ana and I sat and waited. A healer came to our side and recommended that we return to the lake and wait there or walk about the grounds of the Home of Rest. He informed us that we will be called when our dad is waking again. We did as suggested. We strolled in the garden nearby.

"Well, Ana, what do you feel about how dad awoke? Do you feel that he recognized you? I saw that he looked your way quite often. Did you see this?"

Her face lit up when she said, "Oh, Charles, the entire experience was perfect! Each time I am present to welcome someone, it is different. One can never fully anticipate how an individual will respond when they first realize what has happened to them. Dad responded in such a way that tells me that he was prepared by others during the long process of his death. But remember, he is not yet fully awake. You and I will be here to assist, and others will be present also. I was with you a great deal of the time when you were adjusting to the fact of your death and new life here. And you are the one who will be present most of the time during dad's adjustment."

"What about you, Ana? Will you not also be present?"

"Oh, yes of course. But you will be the one most active helping him. I will be available whenever I am called."

After this conversation, we both felt to go back and be with dad. When we arrived, two healers were present attending to dad. He was just beginning to stir awake. The healers quietly moved away and left and we were again alone with him.

When dad opened his eyes, he looked about and saw that we were alone with him. He smiled, sat up and walked to me and gave me a hug.

"I am very happy to see you again, Charles. We have much to talk about, and I have many questions. But I suppose that there is no rush about this. Am I not right?"

I laughed and agreed. "Yes, dad, we do not have a time limit. And we don't use clocks and time pieces of any kind."

I noticed that Dad's eyes kept drifting to Ana. Finally, he said, "You are a beautiful person. I must say that you look like someone I should know, but a name is not coming to me. Charles, will you help me? Should I know this young woman?"

There were soft chairs, and I motioned to them and suggested we be seated. I began to tell dad the circumstances of my own death during the Great War. He added some interesting details and reviewed his memories of the family when they learned of my death. It was good for dad to speak and we to listen; it actually was important for the continuation of his healing process.

I continued with my story. "When I realized where I was, and that I was no longer alive on earth, I recognized the presence of individuals helping me to adjust to my new life here, even as you, yourself, are beginning to realize that a variety of persons come at different times to help you. Well, the lovely young person you see here with me was one of the helpers that stood out among all the others.

"Eventually she and I began to talk and something good happened – something very important to me and will also be for you. Over the course of my recovery and adjustment, which lasted a very long time, it was shown to me by certain teachers, that the young female spending so much time with me is my own sister.

"I was astonished. How could I not be?

"Dad, I did not know. I did not realize that I had a sister that died before me. If I was told, I did not remember. I was ignorant of the fact that I had a sister born about one year before me, and who died one day after her birth. Dad, you are looking at Julia Ana, your daughter."

I hardly finished the last few words, and dad was crying uncontrollably. I went to him and put my arms around him.

"Yes, father," I spoke softly, "it is true; she is your daughter, Ana. She is my sister." I too was crying.

Dad stood and walked to Ana and took her hands.

"Ana, Ana, Julia Ana …" He kept repeating her name as he pulled her up and embraced her. "I do not know what to say. I have no words."

Ana whispered with her angelic voice: "Papa, my dearest father, my dad … I am happy. I love you. I am so very happy to welcome you to your new life. You will discover that this is a life filled with many, many surprises."

Ana is not only a lovely person, she is so very gracious. She took her father's hand and walked with him to a larger chair – a sofa as it is called on earth. It was formed in a curve, just right for the three of us. Dad sat in the middle and Ana and I on either side.

When dad was ready to speak again, he looked at Ana and said "This is a very happy moment being with you and Charles. I had no way of knowing this or even anticipate that this would happen when I arrived here. Before I died I knew that I was dying. I knew without a doubt that I would meet my son Charles again. But I confess that I completely forgot about you, Ana. When you died, both mother and I were devastated. We buried your tiny body, and we also tried very hard to bury the memory of you. It worked for me, but I am not so certain about your mother.

"She grieved a very long time. Sometimes in her sleep I would hear her mention your name – as if she was actually talking to you. While Charles was speaking, a vague memory of you began to surface. And when he spoke your name it was unbelievable to me that you still live, and not only live, but have grown into such a beautiful person. What am I to say? I have no words to use to explain what I am feeling. What joy; what happiness … what a huge and beautiful surprise! What will mother do when she arrives and discovers this blessed truth?"

Ana responded: "Do not worry about this, father, for deep down in her soul mother already knows – although she is not aware that she knows."

I spoke again and told dad the story as I heard it from Ana, that mom, in her sleep-state often visited with Ana when she was an infant, and even later. Through the years her love did not diminish, and she stayed in contact with Ana.

"And then when she passes and arrives here," dad asked, "it will not be as difficult to accept for her as it is for me?"

"Yes, dad, what you have just said is very true," Ana responded.

And I added: "It was difficult for me too dad. But I can't comprehend how it must be for you, for you are her father. Your experience has to be so much more intense. Dad, may I suggest that you will find much help here, not only about this, but other things too. You will continue to adjust and grow as you continue in your new life here. I will help you, as will Ana. But you will discover a host of helpers and teachers present to help and assist."

Ana smiled at her father and asked: "Would you like to go for a walk and explore your new home, or do you prefer to be left alone to rest?"

Dad answered quickly: "By all means, let us go walking. I want to see more of my new world. And I want to walk with you; I want to walk with my daughter and my son."

Together, we walked hand in hand to the garden of flowers.

Joseph, now you have it: the story of the beginning of Andrew's life in a new world. It is a short step that he started some sixty-four years ago. It was an amazing beginning of an adventure in the process of the growth and development of his soul in this world. May his story bless you and your readers with solid information and true inspiration.

Above all, may your soul be enriched and blessed with the continuing inflowing of our Heavenly Father's Great Love –

the greatest blessing of all.
  With our love:
  I am Charles, your loving brother,
  And I am Ana, your ever-loving sister.

## Comment

No matter how many times that I read the above message from Charles and Ana, I shed tears: I do this not from a place of sadness or grief, but happiness. To learn of the reunion between my father and Ana and Charles overwhelms me with awe and fills me with joy and gratitude.

## Tuesday – January 27th, 2015

*I have a desire to sit and write. I am keenly interested in what happened to my dad when he walked hand in hand with Ana and Charles. Did he return to the Home of Rest?*

## My Dad, Andrew – *"Experiences after the Home of Rest"*

Yes, Joseph, you do indeed have many questions. I am here, your father –

I am not giving promise that I will answer all that you ask. After all, we do not intend for your writings to be about me and occupy your time and energy.

You are correct in what you are asking about me. Ana and Charles did indeed escort me to many places of interest. They showed the general countryside where the Home of Rest is located. How we traveled, I am not certain. I did not know then, but of course, I know now from my present vantage point as a Celestial spirit – we traveled by way of thought. Yes, we walked, but travel by way of thought is swift and we are able to cover great distances.

Perhaps I can best describe this in terminology that you understand, namely, your experiences during sleep. One instant you are at a certain location, and the next moment you are elsewhere. Do you stop your dream and ask how you arrive from one place to another? Does it not happen seamlessly and instantaneously?

We saw much, not only land, landscapes, hills and valleys, lakes and streams and people going to and forth, but also quiet villages and larger cities. We visited small communities, and large amphitheaters. In fact, we witnessed a very large gathering of people in one of these where musicians and singers performed great music. While there I felt that I would participate in this. And later, much later, I did.

This leads me to a question you asked. Did I return to the Home of Rest? My answer is no and yes. I mean by this is that I did not return immediately after Ana and Charles showed me things of my new world. But I did return to the Home of Rest to assist as a helper, and later, as one of the healers. Perhaps I may speak of this some other time.

Today I would like to write about my first home – my personal home. I have no way of measuring time and how long it was that I stayed in the Home of Rest, and how long it was that we traveled and was shown sights and places in my new world. But after a long time, Ana and Charles introduced me to one particular home, and even before I was told about the home, somehow, I felt that I was being escorted to my own personal place of residence.

I was happy beyond measure. I felt so completely drawn to this place that I knew before being told that this was my place, and I was home.

We walked a path through trees and a magnificent garden of roses of all colors and fragrances. The trees did not hide the beautiful hills surrounding the home, or the small stream flowing nearby. The home was quite large but certainly not a mansion as some might describe it. I walked through the entrance and entered a large room well-lit by large open windows. There were many comfortable chairs tastefully arranged, but what my eyes were immediately attracted to was the piano and, on a shiny table, a violin and bow! My heart leaped for joy. I played only a short melody on the piano, and the sound was perfect. And I did the same with the violin.

Then we walked to other rooms, and one in particular amazed me – it was a library complete with shelves of books and a large writing desk. Again, my heart was filled with joy and gratitude. I asked: who did this? How did they know? Who thought of this?

Ana came close and answered my questions:

"Father, you created this. Over the years of your life, in one way or another, you dreamed this home into existence, even all the contents. Many people will come here to visit. You will have many friends. They will gather and together you will create music. This is a place for you to study and contemplate, as well as to write. You will also teach here and other places as well.

"You will have many wonderful experiences in this home. There is so much waiting for you to do. But, remember, there is no rush. Everything will come to be when you are ready and desire for it to be. This is a wonderful life, dad: it is only the beginning of your new life."

## Thursday – January 29th, 2015

*I feel something special stirring in my soul, and I have for the last several days. I have said this before and I am confident I'll be saying something similar again: A new door of opportunity awaits me. Is this not also like the promise of the Divine Love? God's Love is waiting. If and when we desire more, it is waiting to fill us. When we realize this, and go to the Father to ask, His love will never be withheld. So, I come again to write, and it will be done.*

*And I ask and wait ... Who is present today to write?*

## Andrew – *"Experience of my progress"*

Joseph, my son, I am here, your father –

I heard your morning prayers and joined with you. You spoke of a desire to write a conversation with me, and so I have come to do this. We never did this when I was on earth.

You asked and I will answer your question. Yes, of course I recall that I asked you a question when we were gathered after the memorial service that we had for your brother, Charles.

How can I forget? In one way or another you carried this question with you through the years. Your readers may like to know what the question is that I asked you.

We were gathered in the living room with all my sons. I asked each one what he planned to do following the war. After this I turned to you and asked a slightly different question: *"Joey, what do you want to do when you grow up?"*

At the time I asked this question you were only a nine-year-old boy, and you did not give answer. I am amazed that you remembered the question, all the way from your childhood into your adult life. Nonetheless, we never sat and had conversation together. You and I never enjoyed conversations as many sons and daughters usually have with their father.

You have it in your heart to do this today. Well, let us try; shall we do it?

*I would like to do this, dad. May I begin by asking you a question?*

Of course, my son. Please ask.

*My question pertains to your present experience as a Celestial angel, and the recent letter I received from you where you described the Home of Rest, and then were introduced to your first personal home. Where was that home located?*

This is a good question, Joseph. I am, as you say, a Celestial soul now, but when I passed I was not in good condition.

As you know, the physical-body pictures the condition of the soul. When our Ana passed as an infant, her frail body did not live past one day. As true as this is, she did not possess many injuries or flaws since she did not accumulate these through many years of living in the physical body. When she came to the spirit-world she healed quickly and became a Divine Angel at an early age.

I, on the other hand, had many years for injuries and flaws to develop very deeply in my soul. My physical body told quite a story of the true condition of my soul. You know this to be a fact, for you were there and saw my physical condition. When I passed I was close to nothing but skin and bones.

I passed into the First Sphere, which has many planes or levels. As you know, some individuals pass into the low regions of this sphere, and quite a few remain there for many centuries. I would say that the location where I passed was somewhere in the middle. I was not a wicked man; I was a Christian and a pastor. I had many beautiful experiences in this regard, and through prayers and worship with music and song, I often experienced God's grace and love.

Nonetheless, I carried deep anger and disappointment within my soul. I kept these and other feelings within me; I never discussed these with anyone. Through the years this anger grew deeper and more intense. And because I assumed my Christian beliefs and faith would remove these feelings and emotions, and they remained, I grew ever more disappointed and resentful. Often, I took my anger out on my children. You remember the whippings you received from my hand. I beat all my children, the girls of course less than the boys. Think about this when you recall the awful appearance of my physical body at the end of my earth life.

*There was mention of healers present to assist when you passed and went to the Home of Rest. What did they do to help you?*

If you are asking, did they go to the root causes of my suffering, namely, my soul, the answer is no. The healers cannot do the work that we ourselves must do. To an extent, the healers assist to remove the influences that are generational, things that I inherited directly from my parents and their parents – what are known as the "sins of the parents." I say, to an extent, for as we grow we assimilate and make these influences our own. The healers cannot and do not remove the choices we made, the willful acceptance of errors and flaws.

Let me give you an example, which may startle you. When I arrived at my own personal home – which, by the way, was located somewhere in a place known by some as Summerland – did you notice how excited I was to see the piano and violin, and the library with the books and writing table?

*Yes, I saw that as a very nice personal touch. I was reminded by this that you had musical talents. And I remember that you had many books in your office, and sermons that you wrote.*

Exactly; you remember correctly. Over the years, however,

though good, they are but external things. They were placed there as helps and instruments to assist my inner healings, and to some extent, they did.

*Dad, excuse me for interrupting, but I really want to ask this before we go further. In an early letter, it was mentioned that you did not become a Celestial soul for many years – in fact, if I recall, mother, when she passed, actually progressed very rapidly, and entered the Celestial Heaven before you. Will you comment on this?*

Yes, of course, Joseph. As you know, mother was much simpler and, in many ways, much purer of heart and soul. With such a large family, she had not the time or inclination to read and study. She loved to sing, but I never encouraged her to do this, as your older siblings have told you.

I was a very strict father and ruled the home in a very disciplinary manner. I beat the children with a whip rather than use the method of talk and reason. I know that you, for example, saw me as a tyrant and bully, rather than a kind and loving father. I was out of control, myself, and ruling with an iron fist did not really help you or the others.

But, mother, she was sweet and tender, the opposite of me. So, when mother passed and came here, she did not come with all the hurt and pain that I arrived with. When she was met by Ana and Charles, she immediately gravitated to Ana. She was like a sponge – a very hungry child; she was a very open and eager soul to learn from her daughter.

I was not so eager and open, and I made it difficult for myself to listen and absorb the simple teachings of my daughter, Ana. Mother was not this way. In no time at all, your mother progressed rapidly. In terms of earth time, it was not more than a year, two at the most, and she progressed to the Celestial Heaven. Charles also helped her a great deal; but it was mainly Ana's influence and teaching that enabled mother to advance so quickly.

I, on the other hand, was very slow. It was not that I did nothing to progress, for I did. But what I did was more in the area of the intellect and the mind. If it were not for mother's presence and great change, I may have progressed to the sixth sphere and remained there a very long time.

*May I interrupt again, dad? How did mother become the influence that helped you to change?*

As I said, I was relatively happy and progressing, but not in the way of the Divine Love. Even though it was explained to me by Ana, that the Divine Love is the greatest thing and the only thing that can make a person at-one with God, I saw no need for this love. I felt no need of the requirement to get this Divine Love. I felt happy and content.

But when mother arrived and I saw the rapid change taking place in her life and appearance, I felt compelled to make inquiry about the change that I witnessed. Mother told me exactly what had been shown me previously by Ana, and to some degree, by Charles. This took place when I was in the Fourth Sphere.

As a result of my investigations, I began a study of the Divine Love: what it is, the purpose for it, and, how to receive it. When I did this, I became extremely interested. Let me say it this way: an interest in the Divine Love was born in me and then, in place of mere interest, a burning desire came into my heart.

Strangely, I felt very uncomfortable where I was in the Fourth Sphere, and subsequently returned to the lower sphere, the Third, where my desires for the Divine Love increased to new levels. In a short time, I advanced to the Fifth Sphere and then quickly to the Seventh Sphere, where our life and attention was completely directed to the grace of our Heavenly Father, and to receiving the abundance of His Great Love. All other attractions and interests became secondary to this one thing: Divine Love became my all in all.

Soon, I was singing a new song of the heart – the victor's song of God's children becoming His children through the Love Substance of His Soul. Singing this song was my passion. One moment I was singing from the heart, and the next moment I discovered I was singing the song of Love – the Divine Love – and I was wearing a new robe in the Celestial Heaven. I beheld people waiting for me. Who was present to greet me? Yes, many Divine Love angels, and among them, Ana, my daughter, Charles, my son, and Julia, your mother and when on earth, my wife.

*And now, today, as you write this letter to your son still on earth, you are a Celestial angel. So, in earth years of time, you have been a Celestial spirit for about forty years – twice the number of years you were in spirit without the Divine Love.*

What you say is not altogether true. I would not say *without the Divine Love*, my son. Many individuals on earth, and here in the spirit-world, have a small amount of the Divine Love but do not have a realization that what they have experienced is the Divine Love of our Heavenly Father. I had a small portion before I died, and I did not lose it when I passed. However, in the spirit-world I did not know this, even after I met my daughter when I arrived and she greeted me.

This is also true about you, Joseph. Only you have become aware of the Divine Love. But before you began to read the messages Jesus gave to James Padgett, back when you were a Christian minister, you had no knowledge that Divine Love exists, and therefore, you did not possess an awareness of the Divine Love in your soul.

Now you do, and you are trying in a variety of ways to help individuals to recognize the presence of the Divine Love. This is not an easy task. We come to encourage you to continue. The messages that you are receiving will become a book, and when distributed and made known, will assist many people.

*Dad, I feel a shift in our conversation has taken place. Are you aware of the title I would like to use for our book of messages? Did you help through your influence to bring the title to my consciousness?*

Yes, of course; but not me alone. We like it; do you?

*I do! But I am also open to a different title, should one be suggested later. The idea of "breaking the silence" describes very accurately what happened the day when you came and, with surprise, interrupted my writings.*

I am smiling, for this is exactly what was intended. We have been silent much too long. You were not expecting me; you were completely unprepared. I like the way it happened, and that I had to wait one more day to write the next letter. It could not have happened in a better way.

*Well, maybe not. You could have used your voice; or, better yet, you could have chosen to materialize in the room where I was sitting at my desk and writing.*

No; to materialize would not have worked. We did not want you to feel fear. We did not need that kind of response from you. But now that you are aware of this as a possibility, we may try this. Prepare yourself!

*Writing this message today has been a wonderful experience. I am busy with other things, but I felt that I had to take time to sit for a message today. I don't mean this in the way of a command to do it, or even a duty, but rather, a deep desire that I sincerely wanted to do. Does this make sense? Will you be writing again? Perhaps a new phase in receiving letters will begin. On the other hand, perhaps I will feel led to work on publishing these messages in a book. I'll try to relax and be patient and wait for directions and suggestions from Celestial guides.*

I have likewise enjoyed our time together today. I want to say that you are receiving my letters quite accurately. We have good rapport. It helps because you maintain carefulness to pray and go to the Father for more of His Divine Love.

I am aware that you still wonder if this is indeed your father who writes. You do not doubt that it is, but you do have some anxiety whether it is more your imagination than the reality of my spirit presence.

Well, I again assure you that it is not the work of your imagination; I am in truth your father. The truth of it is in what you feel. If it did not feel right to you, I am confident you would not continue. I am certain of this.

In addition, if we in the Celestial realms see that you are not receiving our words, but are merely creating words from your creative imagination, you would feel our absence. Inspiration to write would quickly cease. This is what rapport is; it works in both directions.

You and I may write again; but realize that there are others waiting to write also.

I smile when you ask if we are about to begin a new phase in your writing. I smile because is this not what you have been feeling since we started to communicate our messages to you? If you have forgotten this, go back and read again the letters from the beginning, I mean all the way back to March of last year when you received that wonderful message from Martin Luther about the "call for more mediums." Each time that you sit to write it is a new experience – a new door and a new beginning.

This is a good place to close. I will say goodbye for now. Whether it is another who will come to write next, be assured, my son, I am near.

I love you.

Be at peace with the Love that is rich in your soul. I bless you as does our Heavenly Father.

I am Andrew, when on earth, your father – and now your friend and one of your guides.

## Thursday – February 5th, 2015

### Julia: *"I felt the call of your heart"*

Joseph, I am here, your mother –

I come because I felt the call of your heart. I come as your mother; for I am aware of the concerns you have for your family. The physical condition of your daughter – my grand-daughter Julia Rose concerns you. Be assured that we are often with her, I as well as your own sister, Ana. She is never alone, dear son, and she needs to be made aware of this. She has a loving grandmother, and not only one. Her maternal grandmother, Jeanne, is often with her also. Be at peace about this. She is well. You saw a spark of this on Tuesday evening when she was so busy cleaning her bedroom. Do not worry. Love her and do what you know to do to help her.

Now, I want to write about another subject. I was happy that you received several beautiful messages from Andrew, your father. Yes, I think he was surprised when I passed over and took quickly to the teachings about the Divine Love brought to me by Ana, and also to some extent, by Charles. I, myself, could not see my own appearance, but I did see the effect that my presence had upon Andrew and the decision he made to become more sincere and earnest about the Divine Love. My dear daughter was the difference, I believe. I trusted her guidance and teaching, and your father saw how quickly I was being changed.

On earth I was overwhelmed with family duties and had little time for personal development. After I passed into spirit I found out how a caged bird might feel once set free. I experienced true freedom for the first time in my life. And this came mainly with the influence of Ana.

The only thing that consumed my interest were the things being taught by Ana, and the experience of receiving the Love of God into my soul. I felt this Love, and when I realized what it was that I was experiencing, I developed an unquenchable desire for more. And now, consider this, your humble and lowly mother, quickly developed by the Divine Love, rose through the realms of the spirit-world to the Celestial Heavens.

I am still progressing to this day. Though I am not as highly developed as Ana, I am told I dwell in a place in the Celestial world that has no number.

Well, this is all that I wanted to write today, except, of course, to join with others in encouraging you in the work you are doing. And I would add, always love your daughter, and do not worry, for she will soon be completely well.

I love you, my dear son. Continue your earnest prayers to the Father. Love, the Divine Love, will come in overflowing measures.

I bless you with my love.

Your loving mother, Julia.

CHAPTER SIX
# MORE LETTERS FROM FAMILY

## Monday – March 2nd, 2015

*Here it is early Monday morning. I come with a desire for direction and help. I have already prayed, and I pray that I am in good condition to receive a message from my Celestial friends.*

*What is the next step regarding the book of messages that I have received? Are there more siblings who may like to write? I pray that I am open to receive. I wait ...*

## Martin: *"Essential focus of this book"*

Joseph, my friend, this is Martin Luther –
I will not write long, as others are here who desire to write. We feel your pain, for it is anxiety that you are feeling. You received words of advice from a friend, which amounted to a suggestion that the focus of your book be about the experiences of your family. This is a change in your understanding that the focus, as you saw it, be the messages received by James Padgett. We appreciate your understanding, but your friend does have a point worth consideration. The letters from your family will have an audience that mere presentation of the Padgett writings would not have at this time. We in the Celestial Heaven are willing to support this effort of the letters

of your family being a springboard to the larger work that James Padgett did. So, it is that your friend has seen something that you yourself missed.

We advise you to receive further writings from your family. As it is now, your readers may wonder about the seven other siblings in the spirit-world who have not been heard from at this point in the story. Thus far only two siblings have written – Ana, your sister, and Charles, your brother. There are seven others who have already passed, two very recently. Allow your family, who have already written, guide you here. There may be additional stories that would be interesting to your readers. Let us be open, shall we? Let us listen.

I will close now. I, too, shall listen with interest.

Your brother and friend - Martin Luther.

## Mother, Dad, Ana and Charles

Dearest Joseph, we are here: Julia your mother, Andrew your father, and Ana with Charles.

We ask that you pause; breathe deeply. We begin again...

I am here, your mother –

I feel your desire, my son, to know more of the stories of your brothers and sisters.

Let us begin with your sister, Margie. We know how close she is to your heart and feel it would be good for you to hear from her first. We have contacted her and we all are together now. She is crying tears of joy.

Margie, do wish to communicate with Joseph?

## Margie, Bundy, Ted

This is Margie here –

Yes, yes, yes! Oh, I love you Joseph! It feels so good to have this opportunity.

I cannot tell you how beautiful our family is – I mean mother and dad, and Ana and Charles... they are like radiant beams of sunshine reflecting on the Niagara River near our home in Buffalo. The feeling I have when I am with them is of a love so deep and wonderful I cannot contain my enthusiasm and joy. I am so happy.

When I first arrived here I was not in good condition at all. I was met by all four, though I had to be introduced to Ana: I did not know who she was. It was so unbelievable for me to meet her. Oh, what beauty! I cannot describe her radiance, and yet so humble. I discovered that Charles had the same response as mine. I did not want to be away from her presence. And Charles – well, he is so handsome, so full of laughter and smiles. All this made me feel immediately better when I woke to my new life here. I think I acted like a little girl – jumping, skipping and screaming with pure delight. Can you see me doing this?

I may not be making too much sense in what I am trying to say to you. But I am so excited to be here with the family.

No. I do not live with any of them. I have my own place in a very beautiful location.

Yes, I did have a very difficult time at first. I believed myself to be unworthy and it was hard at first to accept that I am loved and accepted. I had a hard time loving myself. My family helped so much, that I think I healed rather quickly.

I am now already in the Third Sphere, I am told. I have only one desire, and that is to be like my family. I want so much to be like Ana and mother, and I am determined to do whatever it takes to do this. They tell me that with the kind of determination that I have it will not be long for me to progress all the way the Celestial world. It is true: I do have a determination that I know that I never had while on earth.

I want to tell you, Joseph, my dear brother, that the books you gave me to read helped me to get to where I am now. I love you, dear sweet Joseph, and when you arrive here, I will be with the others to greet you!

I will say goodbye for now. I feel that I cannot write more at this time. When I am able to do this, I want the opportunity to write again.

With much love – your sister, Margie.

I am here, your sister, Ana –
Oh, Margie, my baby sister; she is so lovely. Yes, she does

play her music here. You should hear her play the piano together with dad. What lovely music they create. It is such a joy to experience. As you know, we do not live together, but we visit often, sometimes alone and sometimes the whole family together.

Now, there is someone else here of our family and he wants to write – your brother, Bundy.

Hello Joe, I am here your brother, Bundy.

Well, I am here, not so jubilant and exciting to listen to as Margie. Yet, in my own way, I am very happy. I cannot tell you how happy I was when I woke in this new life to be greeted by my family, especially mom and, yes, dad, and Charlie and my sister, Ana. To meet her was such a big surprise. And their happiness and joy in seeing me helped me to adjust to my new life here. I want to say that Charles helped me the most. He seemed to take a special interest in me. I feel I would have remained lost without his presence and help. I had so much to learn as well as unlearn.

Yes, I also have seen Ted, and Elmer and Bill. I don't see them as often as I do Charles. He is my best friend!

Where do I live now? Oh, I have a beautiful home that I have been told is in Summerland. Charles has been talking to me a lot about progress and change, but I am having trouble understanding what he means by this. I am probably thick headed. But don't worry, I am happy, and maybe someday soon the things Charles tells me will eventually help me.

*It is not difficult. In fact it is rather simple: Merely ask for help and it will come. Ask for the love and you will experience it.*

Yes, I understand what you are saying. Charles tells me the same thing. I'll experiment; I'll give it a try. I'm sure that Charles will help me to ask for this love.

Well, I think others want to write also. Maybe you and I could have a talk, just you and me. I would like that. I will never forget your help when I was on my death bed at the hospital. You helped me much more than you realize. You didn't see Charles in the room with us when I died. He was there and escorted me to my new life here.

I love you, Joe, and think of you often.
Your brother, Bundy.

I am here, your father –
Well, my son, you have received interesting messages from Margie and Bundy. As you can now see, our family still has connection with one another, even though we are not together as a unit. And you can see the great influence that Ana and Charles have when one of the siblings passes to this new life.

Yes, it is true that Margie and I do play the piano together on occasion. She is very gifted musically.

I realize that you would like to hear from all the others that you have not heard from yet. We will do this another time. We feel you have received enough for today, at least for now. I suggest you go rest; you are more tired than you realize. Soon your family will return from school, and you need to greet them.

We will write again soon, perhaps later today.

We all love you, Joseph. Thank you for calling to us to come to your side.

I am your father, Andrew.


## Tuesday – March 3rd, 2015

*We have had a brief spell of winter: Blustery wind came and the rain finally turned to snow. The wet weather has not dampened my enthusiasm to continue writing messages from the spirit-world. Early this morning I had very good prayer and wanted to record messages, but I was tired and fell asleep. I think sometimes I try too hard and over-extend my reservoir of energy. Spirits often help me to see that I require proper rest. Well, I am here now; it is later in the day, and I pray that I am in good condition to communicate with Celestial friends and family...*

## Charles: *"We have invited Ted"*

Joseph, my brother, this is Charles –

I was present yesterday while you were receiving messages from our sister, Margie, and our brother, Bundy, but I did not have an opportunity to write. I am happy that you received these messages, and, yet, I feel you were a bit disappointed that you did not continue. You must learn to pace yourself. You are not a young person, so you do require frequent rests. Dad sensed this and brought the writing session to a close.

After this, after your rest and throughout the day, I was near and felt your desire to know more about the family. There remain five siblings that have not come yet to write. We have invited our brother, Ted, to come and communicate with you. He is here now and desires to speak with you.

Hello, Joe! I'm here, Ted –
Do you still shoot basketball hoops? Haha: I am laughing!
*Actually Ted, I did a few years ago with my son, James. But I fell and hurt my leg. I am not as agile as I once was. How are you, Ted?*
I am doing quite well. Life in this world is different and it takes time getting used to. Each moment seems new and somehow different. No – we do not have television to watch sports programs. I got over that many years ago.
*What are your activities? What are some things you like to do?*
Well, I study books and nature; I love working in my garden, and I really enjoy visiting with friends, and attend lectures and musical gatherings. Yes, I do often get together with the family. I really like being around them. I don't get to see Bundy as often as I would like. When we are together we really laugh a lot, almost like when we were kids on earth. We tell each other a story and then usually wind up laughing. Sometimes people will gather around us and listen to our tales and join in our laughter.

When I first arrived here I was completely surprised how life here is a big change from earth life. The biggest surprise was that I was greeted by Charles and dad, and mom and our sister, Ana. Gosh, that was a huge surprise. I really forgot all about her.

When I was introduced to her I just could not believe it.

But everyone was so kind it didn't take long to accept that she really is our sister. In appearance she reminded me of Eleanor when she was younger. She also has a lot of mother in her, at least the way I remembered mom from old photos of her.

Oh, now, of course, mother looks so young, and she is very beautiful. And at first I hardly recognized dad; he looks much younger than the old man I had in my memory. So, in a way, I had to be reintroduced to each one; well, not really, except for Ana. Even though each one is now much younger in appearance, somehow, I knew who each one was – except for Ana.

Well, I cannot tell you how happy I was to see Charles again. Wow, that was an awful experience the way that he was taken away from us. I was pretty close to him. Charlie, Marie and I were close in age, and so was Bundy. It hurt deeply when we heard of his death. But that was many years ago. He is here now and smiling at me. What a great person he is. I really like him.

Charles knows a great deal about our life here, and he is my teacher. He teaches me and I do try to listen, but I admit I am slow to learn. Perhaps I am still shy like I was on earth. I can't quite accept that there is more to life here than what I see presented through my eyes and experiences. Charles talks a lot about progress and change; I can understand this up to a point and then the rest goes over my head. I am told my problem is that I do not apply my own effort which would allow change and progress to come. Maybe I am just too content and happy with what I have now, or maybe I am too stubborn to listen to what Charles and others are saying to me. Maybe I am both.

Yes, sometimes I do visit you and study what you are doing. I am surprised that you are still on earth. You have had several close calls with death. And now, here you are, communicating with me. This is as much of a surprise to me as it is to you.

Yes, Charles tells me of the Divine Love, and how it will help me to change and progress. Maybe if I try a bit harder I'll understand what this is.

Yes, I do see the great change and difference in the appearance of dad and mom, and Charles and Ana. Their appearance is brighter than the people who live around me. My friends even notice this when Charles and Ana come to visit me.

You say this is the evidence of the presence of the Divine Love in their lives. Well, Charles tells me the same thing. I don't know why, but when you say it, Joe, something feels different. I wonder what it is.

*I am still here on earth and you are living in the spirit-world. Nonetheless, it is rather simple. Let me try an explanation. On earth, Ted, you were a chemist and a scientist of a sort. You know what chemicals are, and how when they are combined in certain ways, change of substance is the result. This is exactly what happens with the Divine Love, when it is allowed to enter the human, whether mortal on earth or in the spirit-world. The Divine Love is an ingredient straight from God, designed specifically to change the soul – your soul and mine. Ask Charles again about this; he will explain these things much better than me. It is your choice; you are never forced to do it. Try it; allow it to come into your soul, and you will begin to experience the change. Talk openly with Charles and Ana about this. Will you promise me that you will?*

Sure, Joe, I promise you that I will. If there is a possibility that I can change and become like Charles, that would be really neat! I will give it a try. Thank you for sharing this with me. Charles and Ana are here and they are both smiling – almost beaming so I can hardly look at them. Well, maybe there is something to this after all!

Thank you, Joe, for taking your time today to allow me to communicate with you. I can't explain what it is that I am feeling. All I can say is that the things you just shared seemed clearer coming from you. I will study this. Maybe I will find books here to help me. I do like to read.

*Books are great ways to learn and explore. I am certain that the right books are available there; at least this is what I have been informed. Ask; you will find out. But above and beyond this, more importantly, speak openly with mom and dad, and certainly with two great teachers, your brother, Charles, and sister, Ana. Talking with them is much better than a book.*

Thanks again, Joe... This has been a really great experience for me.

I love you, Joe. Hang in there!

I'll talk again with you soon, I hope.

Your brother, Ted.

## Charles: *"Spirit to mortal communication is important"*

Hi again, this is Charles –

Well, that was quite a conversation that you had with Ted. This was a great opportunity for both of you. Sometimes one person can reach another where someone else cannot. These things happen quite frequently. As you know, for me it was our sister Ana.

Because of this conversation today, Ted looks to be more open with Ana and me. Yes, dad and mom are here also, and they are shaking their heads: "Yes!"

This is a blessing to us that we heard this conversation today. We see something that we haven't seen or recognized before. The contact between mortal and spirit is more important than we realized. Your presence and conversation with Ted has really helped him. We saw a light come to his face; we saw an opening of his soul that we had not seen before. This has indeed been a blessing to all of us.

Martin Luther is here and indicating that he wishes to write.

I love you, my dear brother. Thank you for calling to me.

Blessings and love – Your brother, Charles.

## Martin Luther: *"This is a blessed day for all"*

This is Martin here –

I do wish to say a few words.

That was a wonderful meeting between yourself and your brother, Ted.

I realize what this means to you, for you have been troubled about meeting Ted again. You love him, but you had doubts about the possibility of connecting with him. So, the conversation that took place was a very big surprise, and we see evidence already that the communication meant a great deal for him also.

Charles is correct when he said that he saw the soul of Ted opening. Yes, Ted will now be able to receive the influence of love from Ana and Charles. And Ted will now also be open to listen to their teaching and instructions. I am confident that a great change will now begin for Ted.

This has indeed been a blessed day for all.

We are happy for you and for your family. I pray that those who read this will apply this message to their own life, and their loved ones who have passed and are now living in the spirit-world.

Go in peace and with our blessings and the blessings of our Heavenly Father.

I am your brother and friend, Martin Luther.

## Comment

I received an invitation to attend a meeting today and almost did not take time to sit for a message from spirit. After driving my daughter to school, I returned home. I went to my office to take care of a few business items; while doing this, I felt the presence of spirit. So, I cleaned the desk and opened my notebook, and prayed. I breathed deeply and then began to write: the above messages from my family and Martin Luther are the result. I missed the meeting, but I feel content: happy, blessed and grateful.

## Friday – March 6th, 2015

*Today began with an unusual experience. I felt uncomfortable, restless, and wasted several hours doing meaningless things. Finally, already 10:30 a.m., I settled down to pray. I use the word 'settled', but the experience was far from peaceful and quietness. I felt that I was fighting a battle for my soul. I haven't experienced this sort of thing in a very long time. I assumed I was over this kind of experience. Quite literally, I felt negative forces pressing against me: Live spirits in the room fighting to block efforts on my part to pray.*

*However, their scheme did not work. The more 'they' pressed against me the more I was determined to pray with greater earnestness and sincerity. I fought on like this for a long time. I did this using a free and open use of the prayer for the Divine Love that Jesus gave to our brother, James Padgett. Spirit(s) of opposition departed when I came to the part in the prayer about "overcoming evil spirits that constantly surround us and endeavor to turn our thoughts from God to the pleasures and allurements of this world."*

*Well, at this point I realized anew that "it is only we ourselves that can prevent love changing us." So, with increased vigor I persisted in prayer. And when I came to the part in the prayer where we say: "We believe that you are our Heavenly Father, our loving Heavenly Father who smiles on us in our weakness and is always ready to help us take us into your arms of love," I felt that I literally fell into God's waiting arms. I rested calmly, and soon I experienced a deep sleep.*

*After I woke I went immediately to my desk to write:*

## Martin Luther: *"You did nothing to release a thought of negativity"*

I am here, your friend Martin Luther –

I was very near while you prayed and it was truly a very vigorous prayer. Did you literally fight against dark spirits? Yes, indeed you did.

We could have easily removed their influence, had we desired to do this, and if you had called to us for help. But you did not call.

*Why did I not call to you? I usually ask for your presence before I begin to pray.*

Your experience was an expression of your doubt. You have been entertaining negative thoughts, even to the extreme point of destroying the manuscript for your book. Is this not true?

*Yes, what you say is true. This all started two days ago when I was having trouble with my computer. Something happened to cause words to rapidly disappear. I quickly turned off the machine. My first thought was that I did not make a backup of my manuscript, and that I might lose everything that I had done in my manuscript. Then I entertained the thought: Well, what if this did happen? Do I know how to restore the manuscript? If I can't restore the manuscript, do I want to take the time to start all over again? Then I entertained this thought: What is the use? What difference does it really make if I did nothing, and went no further?*

Exactly! The seed-thought of negativity came and you did nothing to release it. The seed grew quickly into a powerful doubt. You have not yet succeeded in overcoming the doubts about the messages you have received from us and your family. You received a note from a friend, though positive, actually fed your doubts.

You assumed you were comfortable with the idea that you have no need for authentication about these messages. Your verification is the messages themselves, you said to yourself. But are they really? Is this enough for you? Is this not the core of your doubt?

And now you have leaped to the conclusion that the world really does not need or even want to see these messages.

I ask you very honest and blunt questions:

Who are you to judge these messages?

Do you know why you have gone in this direction?

Do you see clearly why you fought the battle that you did this morning?

Allow us to help you. We are your friends, not your enemy. Would an enemy desire good for you, and uplift your soul with glad tidings from your family?

Read again all the messages you have received from your family. They have shared their stories with you. Are they not expressions of love and happiness? What did you experience when you read their stories? Were you sad or angry? No: You were happy and filled with joy.

Oh, Joseph, I plead with you to continue to pray. Continue to have longings for our Heavenly Father's Love. You experienced a good thing this morning when you prayed. You felt good, you relaxed, and you became very calm and trusting. This was a great difference from the beginning moments of your prayer when you felt oppressed. This is the real verification and authentication that you are asking for. The authentication is found in the Love – the Divine Love of your Heavenly Father. This is the substance of change that is the most real and authentic thing, both on earth and in the spirit-world. It is true for you, and it is true for your family here in the spirit-world.

This is the message that you need to hear today. Continue and do not cease in the excellent work that you are doing. Help the stories your family is giving to you to go out into the world. Release the book and make it available for others to read. Do not judge how the messages will be received. This is not your work. Your work is to receive and to give.

I have written enough for the present. I pray that what I have written will benefit you and help in the work you have remaining to do.

Be at peace about this. Love yourself as we love you.

I am Martin Luther, your friend and brother.

## Jesus: *"You fought a battle and won"*

I am here, Jesus –

I come to confirm the words of our friend, Martin Luther.

Be strong, Joseph, and be courageous. You have fought a battle of the soul, and you have won.

Do not turn away. A great light awaits you, even as it does for all others who fall into similar temptations of doubt and unbelief. The ones who overcome are those who hear the call of our Heavenly Father and respond to the presence of the Love that is in truth the greatest thing in all the universe. The Father's Love is always your answer and help.

Remember this day. Mark it down. Make record of it. Never forget what happened today. You fought the fight and victory is yours.

Sing for joy; rejoice always in the Love that has set you free.

I am Jesus blessing you as your Heavenly Father blesses you.

### Andrew: *"A touch of heaven in our words"*

I am here your father with all your family –

We are all amazed and grateful for your experience of the battle and victory of your soul, which we may say, included the battle for our stories. If you had failed, and went on to destroy our messages, something of great value to many people would have been lost.

Humanity needs to read our stories. This may seem to be an exaggeration, but it is not. Our stories are bigger than you who receive them, and they are much larger than we who give them.

There is a touch of Heaven in our words. If the reader will allow it, our words will help lift people to a new level of awareness and consciousness.

Very few people on earth are aware of the glories of the Celestial Heavens. We have only touched lightly on the subject of human potentiality. It all resides in the Love that waits close to each human.

You helped yourself out of a pit of darkness by praying the way that you did today. There is greater victory ahead for you and for all people everywhere. Lives can and will change with the addition of the Divine Love. It happened to you, and it will happen for those who read your book and apply what they find in it. We cannot see the future and therefore cannot predict what will happen; but we do know this: Change is possible and change will come. Our stories show hope and real possibilities for change and great happiness.

It is real. Divine Love as the agent of change is real and available. It does change lives. You can begin on earth. Don't wait until you come to the spirit-world.

Martin Luther told you: Do not quit. Allow the Divine Love to do the work of change within you. You have made a good start. Therefore, do not pull away. Continue with your prayers and longings for the Divine Love. And continue with our stories. Publish them so others can hear the call of Love in their heart and choose to listen.

I love you and will help you in every way that I can.

Your father, friend and brother – Andrew.

### Julia: *"Greater experiences of happiness await you"*

This is your mother –

I wish to add my words to those who have already written.

I cannot tell you where I would be today if I had not heard of the Divine Love from our daughter, Ana. I was not a wicked woman, and I suppose I would have remained happy in the place where I first arrived here so many years ago.

But that is just it! I would have remained relatively happy, but I would not have learned about the greater experiences of happiness available to each and every human. I would have missed knowing about the potential for greater happiness, all because I did not know and no one came to tell me.

My story is different because someone cared and came and told me the truth: My own precious daughter, Ana.

I am grateful for the knowledge I was given about the existence of the Divine Love. Once I was given this information, I never turned back. All that you have learned about the Divine Love is true, and the most has not yet been told.

A great new life and world await those who hear the news of God's Great Love: who hear, listen and enjoy the presence of this Divine Love.

I just wanted to say this.

With blessings and love – your mother, Julia.

### Charles: *"Enjoy the feast of Love"*

I also want to add a word; I am your brother –

I was quite surprised when I saw you in action against some pretty nasty looking spirits. Yes, I realize they are also God's children, but at the present time they sure are ugly.

I have seen the likes of these spirits before. Where? you ask. The spirits attacking you reminded me of men I knew years ago when I was a soldier. They love a fight. They hate everyone, especially themselves.

Yes, I did see some of them change for the good when they died and came here. But I also saw some continue in their hateful way of wickedness when they arrived in the spirit-world. They continued to hate and fight for many years. They are miserable and seek to make those around them miserable too.

You did good: You fought off their influence and your cry to the Father for His love brought the result. He answered and Love came. We all saw this, and some of us actually clapped our hands because of the joy we felt when victory came to you. Now you can smile and enjoy the feast of love. Enjoy it!

We all love you deeply and desire only that good will come to you. I am very happy that you will go forward and tell our stories in the book you are writing. It will be an important book.

Continue to fight the good fight. Victory is assured.

With all my love,

Your brother, Charles.

### *Charles adds a short note to his message…*

When you feel malicious spirits around you, please do two things. Firstly, call on your big brother. As quick as a wink I'll be at your side. I looked after you when you were a little boy, and though you are now an old man, I am still your older brother, and I will always take care of you. Call me, please. You do not need to fight anymore battles like you did today, and certainly never alone.

Secondly: Together we will confront the wicked spirits, not only to shoo them away. But we will also teach them about our Father's Love. We do not wish to see them continue in their sufferings. They can change, if they will learn of the presence of help through Love.

This is all I will say at this time.

Again, I truly love you, by dear brother.

Charles.

## CHAPTER SEVEN
# FAMILY GATHERING

**Early Sunday morning – April 19th, 2015**

**Comment**

Today I am reminiscing about family gatherings that often took place at my brother's home on the lake. Bill had a summer home on the shore of Lake George, near a village called Silver Bay, in the Adirondack Mountains of eastern New York State. Every other year the entire family came together for a reunion. Mother last attended a family reunion at Silver Bay in 1968, one year before her passing.

To this date, I have not received a message from Bill; neither from Elmer, Eleanor and Ed.

So, I ask: Can a family reunion in the afterlife be arranged? If this is possible, then I might receive a message from those I have not yet heard from. Would this be a good way to end the messages from my family in this book?

I will now rest and then will pray awhile. After this, I will return and wait for a message from spirit.

**Later the same day –**

*I have returned. Prayer was rich with the presence of love.*

*I will wait now for a response to my comments about a family gathering in the afterlife. Who will come to write? I wait...*

### Ana: *"A family reunion in the afterlife"*

Dearest brother, I am here, your sister, Ana –

Let me say that we have heard your desire to have a family gathering. In truth, we have been considering this very thing: You have successfully felt our influence and prompts. This explains why you have been having the feelings and thoughts you are now expressing with words on paper. So, we thank you for coming today to write.

With me are dad and mother, as well as Charles.

We have already contacted Margie, Bundy and Ted. They are so excited they hardly know what to say. Yes, they are willing attend such a gathering.

We have also been in contact with those you mentioned that have not yet had the opportunity to communicate with you: Elmer, Bill, Eleanor and Ed. Each one has expressed interest and a desire to gather in such a meeting, or as you call it, a family reunion. And their desire to do this increased when they learned that you wish to record this event through writing a message for your book.

### Ana continues: Preparation for the Reunion

Now, how do we plan to do this?

As you know, we each live in a different location in the spirit-world and are at different levels of development. Those with lower development cannot possibly visit our homes in the Celestial Heaven. And, if we of the Celestial Heavens go to them, where will we go? Should it be the lowest place, or somewhere between?

The solution is actually quite simple – not easy by any means – but possible and simple.

We of higher soul development are able to "lower" our energies (or vibrations). And our Celestial friends with similar development will be present to assist. If we did not do this, Ed and Eleanor, for example, would not be able to see us.

Each one of lower soul development will require assistance. We that have Celestial soul development will maintain a certain level of vibration for the entire group so that all may see each other and enjoy our time together. This will be done seamlessly so that none need be aware of the "mechanics" of this operation. We only share this with you for your information and those reading your book.

When will this happen? When will we gather for this family reunion?

It is happening now, as you write.

We are in a place which all will enjoy. We will help each individual to relax and feel that all is well and peaceful. The feeling of welcome will enable all of us to enjoy one another's company. It will be a happy experience.

The location is – as you have already imagined it – a place with many trees and flowers, soft rolling hills, near the water, a lake. It has a pavilion available, and many soft chairs placed about for relaxation and very conducive for conversations with one another.

You ask: Has everyone already met each other? Have those that recently arrived in spirit met me, dad and mother, and Charles? Have they met their other siblings?

The answer is yes to these and other questions you ask. So, there is no need for introductions. However, this will be the first time that everyone is all in one place at the same time. It will be a beautiful experience, and we pray that it will be a happy time for all.

### Ana Continues: Coming together for the reunion

There was much activity associated with the family gathering. Each one arrived separately. There was no immediate appearance of all at one moment. Ed and Eleanor, actually had escorts: spirit guides that assisted them to our location. These guides remained separate and out of sight during the gathering, yet close enough to assist.

Mom, dad, Charles and I arrived first in order to greet the

others as they arrived. Each person arrived in order by how long they have been in the spirit-world: according to the date they passed from their earth life.

Thus, the first to arrive was Bill, who died in 1989, and has been in the afterlife 26 years. Bill did not require a visible guide, for he is quite acclimated to the means of travel here. When he arrived, we had a chance to chat before the next person arrived, which was Elmer.

Elmer is the oldest sibling, and he died in 1996: he has been in the spirit-world 19 years. Elmer also did not require the assistance of a visible guide. The six of us had quite a nice conversation while we awaited the next arrival. Both Bill and Elmer understood that other siblings would arrive according to the number of years they have been here.

So, the next to arrive for the reunion was Ted, who died in 2005, and has been about 10 years. Ted also did not require an escort, finding his own way and arriving with no difficulty. The happy reunion was beginning to develop: three siblings recently joining Charles and me in the spirit-world. Conversations continued as we waited the next arrival.

Bundy came the way alongside the lake: he died in 2008 and has been in the afterlife a little over 7 years. He did not require an escort but welcomed assistance and so he had a travel companion. He added his wit and humor to our conversation.

Margie arrived soon after Bundy. She died in 2011 and has been in the spirit-world 3 short years. Margie has already experienced development, but, still, welcomed a travel companion and escort to the location of the family reunion. Everyone greeted her and she quickly joined our conversation.

The next to arrive was Ed, and he required an escort to lead him to our location. Ed is the fourth-born sibling, born in 1920 and died in 2014 at the age of 94. He has been in the spirit-world less than a year (9 months as of this writing). Our greetings to Ed were hearty and sincere.

Very soon after this, we welcomed our eldest female sibling, Eleanor, born in 1919. She died in 2014 at the age of 96 and has been in this spirit-world only 6 months. Eleanor was lovingly greeted by all, and, of course, required a guide to help her to our location.

All the siblings who have passed from earth life were now all present.

Soon after Eleanor arrived, I noticed that persons began to walk about, and "groups" began to form. Individuals began to gravitate to those they wanted to continue special conversations, based on interests and concerns.

I saw Bill walk together with mom and dad, and it was apparent that they were already in deep conversation. I looked and saw Elmer together with Charles, Ed, Ted and Bundy.

I was with Eleanor and Margie. I will tell you why: If you have looked at a family birth chart you would notice that Eleanor was a 5-year-old girl when I was born, and she has vivid memories of both my birth and death. So, she attached herself to me quickly. And, Margie, well, she is so sweet and of tender heart: she loves her sister Eleanor very deeply and has held her hand since Eleanor arrived here for our reunion.

### A brief message from dad:

Bill and I, with mother, were in conversation about several things. One had to do with his continuing questions and concerns about the subject of the Divine Love in comparison to basic church doctrines and dogmas. As you know, he and I were pastors in the church on earth – Bill for more years than me, and many more years than you, Joseph. Bill continually asks mother the same questions, only on a more practical and personal level. He also has a great many questions about the soul: what it is, and also soulmates, and why mother and I do not live together. Well, we discuss these very same things whenever we are together.

### A brief message from Charles:

We (dad, mom and Ana) are referring here to the law of attraction, for it is evident that we formed three small groups each around a common interest. In our group, Ed and Elmer desired to hear about my experience in the war, and how it was for me to get rid of hate and anger. We were all in WWII.

Actually, however, Ed and Elmer, and Ted and Bundy, mostly wanted to be near me in order to hear more of my story of how I progressed to my present home in the Celestial Heaven. Ed had heard nothing about this, knew nothing about the Divine Love, and so he was very attentive to the questions asked by Elmer, Ted and Bundy. But mainly each one wanted to stand close to me: to be near the brother that they mourned so many years ago. They were thankful to be together with me.

### *Ana returns to her narration:*

As if on cue, all of us began to walk slowly toward the pavilion, where there were eleven comfortable chairs arranged in a circle. As we moved closer to the chairs, it was quite evident that we selected our chair near the person in the small group we were walking with.

If you drew a circle on a piece of paper, I will show you where we sat within the circle:

At the top of the circle on your paper, facing the center, there was mother, dad and Bill. Mom is to the right of dad, and Bill to dad's left. Continuing clockwise, Elmer is next to Bill (on his left), and then in order, Ed, Bundy, Charles and Ted. Still going clockwise, Margie is to the left of Ted; next, Eleanor and then myself (Ana). This completes the circle, with mother to my left.

When we were all seated and comfortable, we began the next phase of the reunion: communicating with you.

## GATHERED TO COMMUNICATE WITH JOSEPH

Come, then, Joseph, come and join our family reunion in the world beyond yours.
*Is everything ready?*

Yes, Joseph, I am here, Ana –
Everyone is present; they have been here for a while. It is a joyful event. Everyone is happy and enjoying one another's company. I have already informed them that you will be

present to record the event.

They are smiling: it has become quiet. Those you have not yet received a message from are particularly quiet, not knowing what to expect or to do. Well, this is new for all of us, and we are not so certain what to expect and what to do. I am smiling; this is helping all of us to relax and enjoy what is unfolding.

They cannot see you, of course ... except some are waving their hands to show that they are saying "Hi, Joseph." They are shaking their heads "Yes."

*Who?*

Well, mom and dad, and Charles.

Don't worry. Joseph, we cannot see you clearly. We see only a 'misty' image.

Alright; let us proceed.

Bill and Elmer are laughing heartily; so are Bundy and Ted and Margie. Everyone is smiling. Margie and Eleanor are sitting close and holding hands.

*"Hello everyone," I speak, yet not really knowing if they hear me.*

Ana: Everyone laughs and they say aloud: "Hello, Joe!"

### Dad is smiling and speaks first:

"Joseph, what a great idea this is to gather the family in one place. Yes, it is true that we are individuals and each has his or her own life here, but we recognize and love each other as the family that we were and are."

### Mother responds with a brief message:

"Joseph, we are not asking you to leave earth and your family, but we do want you to know that we all love you and look forward to your coming here to be with us someday. I want to say that Eleanor looks very good and happy, as does your brother Ed."

*Joseph: This is hard for me; it's a new experience. I would like to hear from each one. Does everyone feel comfortable to try this experiment?*

### A message from Bill:

"Joe, I think we are all fine. Please know that I am happy here, and I am in the process of learning so much. I have not quite gone over to the way of the thought about the Divine Love that you and others are so taken with. But I will say this: I admit that this gathering is opening me to things I had not seen or thought about. It is such a positive experience, a good feeling to see us all together. It is greater than I anticipated: even as good as the family reunions we had at our home on Lake George.

It is still hard for me to accept that the beautiful young lady here is my kid sister, Ana.

This is taking some time, for me personally, to get used to. And that's something we have plenty of here: time!

I want to say to you personally, Joe: I hope I can come to you privately and talk. We will make this happen: Alright? I want to do this."

*Joseph: "Yes, Bill; I would love to do that and I will look forward to it. Eleanor, I am very happy you are present. How are you?"*

### A message from Eleanor:

"I am fine, Joe. Thank you for asking. I am one very surprised person! As you know, I didn't think anything like this existed. I thought that when I died, that was the complete end of everything for me. So, you can imagine how I felt when I woke and saw myself in this beautiful world.

Yes, I realize now, that you could have talked to me about this, but I know I would not have listened, especially to you, Joe.

Yes, Marie did try to tell me of these things, but I would not listen to her.

I had my mind made up: I was very closed minded about this.

But now here I am! And I am thoroughly enjoying the experience. I am finding that there is so much to see and do.

Just think about this: I can walk under my own power. I don't require the use of a 'walker.' I can even run if I want to...and I have! I look and feel younger already.

And, wow, I love my little sister, Ana. She is so beautiful and such a lovely and kind person. I admire her so much, and I love looking at her with mom. And daddy: what can I say? It is really him; I do recognize him, and yet he is also very different. He is handsome and a true gentle man.

Like Bill said, I hope you and I will talk soon in private. I want my family to know I am really fine. I have so much to talk about."

*Joseph*: *"Thank you Eleanor; I hope so too. Elmer: I haven't heard from you. How are you?"*

### A message from Elmer:

"Hi kid brother. I cannot see you. But I can feel your presence. Well, you and I had some very deep conversations over the years. But we didn't get to see each other much before I died, or, as you and others say, passed.

To tell the truth, I feel like a little boy. I am finding there is so much for me to learn about my life in this world.

I live in a nice home, not too far from Bill. I probably see Bill the most, but I do enjoy seeing the others too.

I want to say I really appreciate this gathering. I'm absorbing what I see and hear; it is already making a difference how I think about things.

For example, I did not know we can communicate with those still living on earth. This is good to know.

I'm very happy to see Ed again. I think I'll be visiting with him a lot in the near future. And it is so good to see Eleanor here. What a time she is having. I am really happy for her.

I like what she said about Ana. Goodness, I never expected to see and meet her here! Surprises: This is what life here has been for me thus far.

And, now, to learn that I can communicate with you is simply amazing. What is next?

Well, I will close, but I also would like the chance to meet with you personally. I have so much I'd like to say and tell my family still on earth…"

*Joseph*: *"Thank you Elmer. And Ed: How are you?"*

### A message from Ed:

"What a fantastic experience this is! To be here with family, and also to communicate with you! How is this possible?

Okay: I understand. I will talk with Ana and Charles about this. And maybe even dad and mom.

What will I find out next? You know me, Joe; I will ask questions and investigate until I find the answers I seek.

I am feeling fine; thank you for asking. But, wow, I had a heck of a time getting here. Some say it took a long time for me to wake up.

Oh, well, I have nothing but time on my hands to learn what this new life is all about.

It is hard for me to accept that the young man I'm looking at is in fact my dad. Goodness, what happened to you, dad?

And I'm looking around at all of you: You all look amazing, younger and healthy! How can this be? Some of you know that I am very sentimental, and right now I feel that I am going to cry: I love you all!"

### Ana narrates:

Ed shouts to all: "I love you!"…and everyone laughs.

Mother stands up and walks over to Ed and gives him a long hug. This is so beautiful to watch.

After this everyone stands and a big group hug begins to happen: including me (Ana).

*Ana returns to continue her narration:*

Everyone is happy, and those who had not written shout greetings to you: Charles, Bundy, Ted and Margie.

The reunion continues: the family is experiencing a great amount of happiness in the presence of love.

And, now, Joseph, my narration of the family reunion ends. With all my love,

I am your loving sister – Ana.

## FOLLOWING THE FAMILY REUNION

*A brief message from Martin Luther:*

I am here, Martin Luther –

If I may, I would like to add a comment or two.

First, let me say that I was present during the entire family reunion, unnoticed of course. Much of the time I stood near your brother, Bill, in order that he might feel my presence. As I have shown great interest in you, Joseph, I would like you to know that I also have a similar interest in Bill.

Yes, there were many Celestial friends present during this gathering; more than you can possibly imagine.

This gathering of your family was a unique and unusual event: fruits of it will show in short order. We are happy for your family, especially for the two who are new to the spirit-world and the beginning of their new life.

Should a meeting of this nature not be repeated, each individual will have an enduring memory of it. It will be the catalyst and influence for change and greater soul development for all. The presence of your mother and father, with your sister, Ana, and Charles, presented a wonderful picture and ideal for your other brothers and sisters.

We remain very interested in the progress of your book. Do not be too concerned if it is found to be imperfect in its final production. Perfection is a wonderful ideal working toward, but usually not fully achieved in your earth experience.

Keep your purpose clear, which is to experience the Divine Love, and along with this to generate interest in the Divine Love with as many people as possible.

We love and bless you,

Martin Luther with many other Celestial friends.

# PART THREE

PADGETT & FINAL RESPONSE

CHAPTER EIGHT
# ONE HUNDRED YEARS AGO

TESTIMONY OF JAMES PADGETT

In his own words, James wrote his testimony. The following is an excerpt from a letter that James Padgett wrote to Dr. George H. Gilbert of Dorset, Vermont, dated December 26th, 1915:

> First permit me to state that I am a practical lawyer of 35 years' experience, and as such not inclined to accept allegations of fact as true without evidencing proof. I was born and reared in an orthodox Protestant church (Methodist) and until quite recently remained orthodox in my beliefs – that upon the suggestion being made to me that I was a psychic, I commenced to receive by way of automatic writing, messages from what was said to be messages from the spirit-world, and since that time I have received messages upon many subjects, but mostly as to things of a spiritual and religious nature, not orthodox, as to the errancy of the Bible.
>
> I have not space to name the great number of the writers of these messages, but among them is Jesus of Nazareth. I will frankly say that I refused for a long time to believe that these messages came from Jesus, because God, while He had the power, as I believed, would not engage in doing such a thing; but the

evidence of the truth of the origin of these messages became so convincing, not only from the great number and positiveness of the witnesses, but from the inherent and unusual merits of the contents of the messages, that I was forced to believe – and now say to you that I believe in the truth of these communications with as little doubt as I ever believed in the truth of a fact established by the most positive evidence in court.

The great object of these messages from Jesus, as he wrote, is to make a revelation of the truths of his Father. He asserts that the Bible does not contain his real teachings as he disclosed them while on earth – that many things that he said are not therein contained, and many things that are ascribed to him therein he did not say at all -- and he wants the truths made known to mankind. And I must say that many of these truths which he has written I have never before heard of, and I have studied the Bible to some extent.

James Padgett continued to practice law until his death in 1923. He was not surrounded with a large group of devoted followers and did not become the leader of a new religious movement. To this day, the name "James Padgett" is not widely known.

James developed into an extremely successful medium for receiving spirit communications. His friend, Dr. Leslie Stone, made the statement that James had received as many as 2,500 messages from the afterlife – which to date has not been verified.

It is important to note that James Padgett did not publish his writings. After his death, this was accomplished by his friend, Dr. Stone. The publishing work was slow and tedious. The first book of messages recorded by James Padgett was not published until nearly twenty years after Padgett's passing. And the final publication of the entire body of the Padgett Messages in four volumes was completed in 1972. The four volumes have the title "True Gospel Revealed Anew by Jesus." In addition to Jesus, there were over two-hundred different individuals in the spirit-world who came to write messages through James Padgett. It is a monumental body of work in the history of mankind. The four volumes are available through the Foundation Church of the New Birth, P.O. Box 6, Williamsville, New York (14321).

Many people reading this book have never heard of James Padgett and his writings. For the purposes of this book, selections of a few writings from the Padgett Messages, primarily excerpts, are included as an introduction to the work of James Padgett.

## SELECTION OF MESSAGES
## RECEIVED BY JAMES PADGETT

**Helen Padgett**: *"The experience of her passing"*
December 9th, 1914

When I realized that the time had come for me to go, I did not fear to do so, but calmly waited and thought that all my sufferings would soon end. And when my spirit left the body I commenced to feel as if I was rising out of it and that I was going upward to the place that I had so often heard my father speak about. But I had scarcely awakened to the fact that my spirit had left the body before your mother had me in her arms and was trying to tell me that I had nothing to fear or cause me to feel that I was not with those that loved me.

She was so beautiful that I hardly realized that it was she, and when I commenced to see that I was no longer in my body, I asked her not to leave me but to take me with her to where she lived. She told me that I could not go there, but that God had prepared a place for me to go to, and that she would accompany me and show me the truth of my future existence. I went with her, and she took me to a place that was very beautiful and filled with spirits who had recently passed over.

She did not leave me for a long time, and when she did, your father came to me and said, "I am Ned's father and want to help you to realize that you are now in the spirit-world and must not let the thoughts of the earth keep you from getting in a condition to learn that all of us are only waiting for the love of God to help us to higher and better things."

Your grandmother soon came to me and told me who she was and was so beautiful and bright that I scarcely could look at her, for her face was all aglow with what seemed to me to be a heavenly light; and her voice was so sweet and musical that I thought she must be one of God's angels that I had read about in the Bible. She told me of the things that God had prepared for me, and that He wanted me to love Him and feel that He loved me.

But after a while I commenced to think that I must be deceived in my sight and hearing, and was still on earth, and needed only my body again to know that I was still a mortal. Some time elapsed before I really became conscious that I was a spirit and was not on earth; for when I tried to talk to you, as I did, you would not listen to me and turned away from me as if you did not see or hear me. After a short time your mother and father came to me again, and tried to persuade me that I must not continue in my belief that I was still of the earth, but must believe that I was in spirit life, and needed only the things of the spirit to make me more contented. So, you see, I was so very fortunate in having your dear parents and grandmother welcome me when I passed over. If they had not received me I do not know to what condition of fear and distraction I might have been subjected. No spirit can learn the truth of the change, unless in some way helped by others. So you see, when you come over I will be there to receive you and love you so much that you will never have to go through the period of doubt that I did. Your father is also waiting to receive you, and in fact, all your spirit band have agreed that when you come, you will have nothing to fear for want of help and love.

**Ann Rollins:** *"He is God of love to everyone"*
January 8th, 1915

[Note: *Ann Rollins is the grandmother of James Padgett.*]

He is God of love to even the vilest sinner, and when such a sinner turns to Him and prays for forgiveness and love he gets them both.

Let me tell you further that the love of God, when it enters into the soul of a man is sufficient to wash away all sins, and make that soul happy and joyful.

Not even the most evil man who is guilty of the greatest sin need think that he cannot be pardoned, and made happy and brought into harmony with God.

The light that men need is not one of belief in any ordinance of the church or creed or doctrine, but simply that a belief in God's love and the exercise of the will of a man accompanied with a desire to obtain that love, with an earnest prayer to the Father, are all that is necessary to bring true happiness and salvation.


**Jesus:** *"God is a God of Love"*
March 3rd, 1915

God is a God of love, and no man can come to Him, unless he receives the love of the Father in his soul.

As men are inclined to error and the violation of God's laws, they can be redeemed from that sin and error only by obtaining this love; and that can be obtained only through prayer and faith in the willingness of God to bestow this love upon whomsoever may ask for it.

I do not mean that there must be formal prayers or compliance with any church creeds or dogmas; but the prayer that is efficacious is that which emanates from the soul and earnest aspirations of a man.

So, let men know, that unless they have the real soul longings for this love, it will not be given to them; no mere intellectual desires will suffice. The intellect is not that faculty in man that unites him to God.

Only the soul is made in the likeness of the Father, and unless this likeness is perfected by a filling of the soul with the Divine Love of the Father, the likeness is never complete.

Love is the one great thing in God's economy of real existence. Without it, all would be chaos and unhappiness; but where it exists, harmony and happiness also exists. This I say, because I know from personal experience that it is true.

Let not men think that God is a God who wants the worship of men with the mere intellectual faculties; that is not true. His love is the one thing that can possibly unite Him and them.

This love is not the love that is a part of man's natural existence. The love that men have, who have not received a part of the Divine Love, is not sufficient to make them one with the Father; nor is that love the kind that will enable them to enter the Celestial spheres and become as the angels who are filled with this Divine Love, and who do always the will of the Father. This love is found only in the souls of those who have received it through the ministrations of the Holy Spirit, the only instrument of God's workings that is used in bringing about the salvation of men.

I have seen the operations of the Spirit upon the souls of men and know what I tell you to be true. No man must rest in the assurance that any other instrumentality or medium than the Holy Spirit will enable him to obtain this Love. He must not rest in the thought that without this he can become a part of God's Kingdom, for no love but this Divine Love can entitle and qualify him to enter that Kingdom.

When on earth I taught the doctrine of salvation only through the workings of the Holy Spirit in fulfilling the commandments of the Father. Mere belief in me or in my name without this Love will never enable any man to become the possessor of this Love. Hence the saying; "that all sins against me or even against God's commandments may be forgiven men, but the sin against the Holy Spirit will not be forgiven them, neither while on earth nor when in the spirit-world." This means that so long as a man rejects the influences of the Spirit he sins against it, and such sin prevents him from receiving this Divine Love; and hence, in that state he cannot possibly be forgiven, and be permitted to enter into the Celestial Kingdom of the Father.

God's Love is not that which needs the love of man to give it a Divine Essence, but on the contrary, the love of man in order to become Divine in its nature, must be completely enveloped in or absorbed by the Divine Love of the Father. So, let man know that his love is but the mere shadow of what the Father's Love is, and that so long as he refuses to receive this Love of the Father, he will be compelled to remain apart from the Father, and enjoy only the happiness which his natural love affords him.

I am so certain that all men may receive this Love, if they will only seek for it in the true way and with earnest desire and faith that I know it is possible for all men to be saved. But men have the great gift of free will, and the exercise of that gift towards the seeking and finding of this Love seems to be a difficulty that will prevent a large majority of the human race from receiving this great redemptive boon.

### Helen Padgett: *"Ever increasing happiness"*
March 3rd, 1915

The message of the Master was so full of things that should make men think and work to get this Divine Love that he spoke of. I am happy to say that I have it now to a considerable degree, and the more I get of it the happier I am.

I thought that I was happy when I entered the third sphere, and more so in the fifth, and then supremely so in the seventh, but, really, I did not know what happiness was, until I got into my present home in the Celestial Heavens; and I suppose as I go higher, the happiness of each succeeding progressive sphere will be so much greater than that from which I progressed.

But, of course, the Master has been the great teacher, whose love and power have helped me more than all the others. He is so wonderful in love and wisdom that I almost adore him, although, he says that I must worship only God, and I follow his directions.

My experiences here are so wonderful that I hardly realize

what it all means.

My time in the spirit-world has been so short, and yet, the wonderful knowledge of spiritual truths and the great happiness that I have received, cause me to wonder in amazement that such things could be.

## Jesus: *"The Influence of Divine Love"*
March 6th, 1915

This Divine Love is also the influence which makes men on earth think and do that which makes for peace and good will among men. It is not possessed by all men, in fact, by comparatively few, yet its influence is felt over nearly the whole earth. Even those who have never heard of my teachings, or of my Father, enjoy the benefit of its influence – in some kind of belief or faith in an overshadowing spirit of great power and watchfulness. I know that this is true, for I have visited all parts of the earth, and have looked into men's hearts and found in them some elements of belief, which evidenced that this great love was influencing these unenlightened people. So, notwithstanding the fact that my gospel is not preached to every creature, as I commanded when on earth, yet this love of the Father is everywhere and all pervading.

Only this Divine Love can change the natural man into a man having the divine nature in love that the Father has. I do not mean that man, even though he be filled with this love to the highest degrees, will ever become a god and equal to the Father in any of his powers or attributes. This cannot be, but this love will make him like the Father in love and happiness and harmony. This love has no counterpart in all creation, and comes from the Father alone. It changes not, nor is ever bestowed on anyone who is unworthy, or refuses to seek for it in the only way provided by the Father.

My experience in these Celestial Heavens is that this love has the power to change the most hardened sinner into a true child of God, if only through faith and prayer such sinner will seek for it. Let this love take possession of a man or spirit, and its power to purify and change the heart of that man or spirit never fails.

## Ann Rollins: *"The coming of the Divine Love"*
June 1st, 1916

I will not write much in detail, as to what man himself should do in order to bring into operation the workings of the Holy Spirit, but merely say, that he must pray with the sincere longings of his soul for the inflowing of the Father's love, and have faith that such love is a real thing and that it comes to him in response to his prayers.

As to the truth that this love is waiting for all mankind, no matter where the individuals of the race may be, and that they can receive this love even though they have never heard of the plan of salvation as declared by Jesus.

God intended, when He rebestowed this love, that every human being as well as spirit should have the opportunity to obtain it, and that the manner in which it might be obtained should be made known to all mankind; and in carrying out this intention he specially selected Jesus for this work, who, through his own teachings to mankind, should learn of it.

Of course during the short ministry of Jesus on earth it was impossible that all men should learn this through the teachings of himself or of his disciples; and hence, the spirits of the world of spirits were permitted to hear these teachings, and come into the knowledge, and then, when they should obtain this love, to teach it to mortals and spirits, which they did, and have been doing ever since.

And just as on earth, where men have refused to listen to those in mortal life who have attempted to teach them of things religious, so in the spirit-world many spirits have and are refusing to listen to the teachings of other spirits, who have the knowledge and possession of this great love. And mortals also have failed to respond to the impressions which spirits have been trying to make upon them as to this truth, and, as a consequence, were unable to open up their soul perceptions. And many mortals, as well as spirits, have never received the benefit of the great gift of rebestowal. And yet, many have responded to these impressions, and even while on earth have had the inflowing of this love to a more or less extent, although they may not have been conscious of the fact in such a definite manner as to know that what they had received was a portion of the Divine Love.

### Jesus: *"Soul transformation – Leaven in the dough"*
June 27th, 1916

When man takes on the divine nature and becomes absorbed in the essence of the Father, he then becomes like the Father, and whatever his image to the Father may have been when he was mere man, now he becomes the real substance, and limitations of possibilities become removed, love sees no ending, and intellectual development no boundaries, happiness no limitations, and immortality becomes a thing of knowledge, and the soul a new creature having the divine essence of the Father; and until this new creation has taken place, and the transformation becomes a thing of reality, and the soul be made at-one with the Father, man cannot enter into the Kingdom of Heaven. Then, no longer man but now an angel.

Now, all this can be accomplished only by the operation of the new birth – that is, the inflowing into the soul of man of the Divine Love of the Father. This love contains the essence of God's divinity, and when man obtains it he is then of the same essence as the Father, and for the first time becomes a part of the divine, and fitted to inhabit the Celestial Heavens.

In no other way can man partake of this nature; and it does not require much reasoning to show the logical truth of this statement, for man in his earthly affairs, and in his material experiments in producing compounds from elements, applies the same principle that I assert in my statement, The dough cannot be leavened unless leaven is placed in the batch.

So, you see that without this Divine Love entering into the soul it will be impossible for the natural man to become the divine angel.

Beliefs and creeds and doctrines and sacrifices cannot work

this transformation, and even though the beliefs may be without doubt, and the creeds and doctrines satisfactory, and the sacrifices without end, yet they will all be futile to change the soul of the mere man into the soul of the divine angel.

### John: *"Divine Love is the greatest thing in the world"*
August 5th, 1916

Divine Love is the greatest thing in all the world, and the only thing that can make man at-one with the Father, and change the soul of man as it has existed since his creation into a divine substance filled with the essence of the Father.

There is nothing else in all the universe of God that can cause man to become a new creature, and an inhabitant of the Father's kingdom; and when men possess this love, then they possess everything that will make them not only the perfect man, but the divine angel.

Then men will understand the moral precepts of brotherly love, and also the Father's oneness, and they will not have to seek for other help in order to bring into the life of the human race those qualities that will bring to it peace and good will.

Then will every man know that every other man is his brother, and be able to do unto each as he would have the other to do unto him, and this without effort or sacrifice on his part. For love worketh its own fulfillment and all its beneficence floweth towards the fellow-man as falls the dews from heaven. Envy and hatred and strife and jealousy and all the other evil qualities of man will disappear, and only peace and joy and happiness will remain.

It is so abundant that it may be possessed by all men, by the mere seeking and the sincere longing for its inflowing. But man must understand that it is not his by matter of right, nor is it ever forced upon him, but comes only in response to the sincere earnest prayer of a soul that is filled with longings for its coming.

This love comes not with observation of mere moral rules, or with good deeds and the exercise of the natural love of a man towards his fellows, because no man can possibly merit it by any deeds or acts or kindness of heart that he may have. All these things are desirable, and they work out their own rewards, and bring the happiness and peace that result from good thoughts and kind deeds; but all these do not bring into the soul of man this great love.

It is the Father alone who bestows this love, and only when the soul is opened up to its reception can it possibly find its home in that soul.

It is greater than faith or hope, because it is the real substance of the Father, while faith and hope are the qualities which a man may possess by his own efforts, and which are given him that he may realize the possibility of obtaining this love. They (faith and hope) are merely means; love is the end and fullness of their exercise.

But men must not believe that all love is the Divine Love, for it is very different in its substance and qualities from all other loves.

All men have, as a part of their possessions, the natural love, and they need not pray for a bestowal of that (although since it has become defiled by sin, it needs to be purified and freed from this blight, and the Father is ever willing and ready to help men obtain this purification).

But this Divine Love is not a part of man's nature, nor can he obtain or possess it except he seek for it.

Divine Love comes from without and is not developed from within. It is the result of individual acquirement, and not the object of universal possession.

It may be possessed by all; it can be possessed by only a few; and each man must determine for himself whether it shall be his.

With God there is no respect of persons; neither is there any royal road to the obtaining of this love. All must pursue the same way, and that way is the one that Jesus taught – the opening up of the soul to this love finding a lodgment therein, which can be brought about only by sincere prayer and longing for its inflowing.

This love is the life of the Celestial Heavens, and the only key that will unlock the gates; and when the mortal enters therein, all other love is absorbed by it. It has no substitute, and is, of itself, a thing apart. It is of the essence of the divine; and the spirit which possesses it is divine itself.

It may be yours; it may be all men's – and it may not. You must decide that question for yourself … Not even the Father can make the decision for you.

## Jesus: *"Prayer and Longing for the Divine Love"*
December 2nd, 1916

I merely want to say a word for the benefit of you and your friend, and that is, that I have listened to your conversation tonight, and find that it is in accord with the truth; and the influence of the spirit is with you both. Continue in your line of thought and in prayer to the Father, and, also, in your making known to others, whenever the opportunity arises, the importance of seeking for and getting the Divine Love.

As your friend said, the only prayer that is necessary is the prayer for the inflowing of this love. All other forms or real aspirations of prayer are secondary, and of themselves, will not tend to produce this love in the souls of men …

Let your prayer be as follows:

Our Father, who is in heaven, we recognize that you are all holy and loving and merciful, and that we are your children, and not the subservient, sinful and depraved creatures that false teachers would have us believe. We know that we are the greatest of your creations, and the most wonderful of all your handiworks, and the objects of your great soul love and tender care.

We know that your will is that we become at-one with you and partake of the great love which you have bestowed upon us through your mercy and desire that we become, in truth, your children through love and not through the sacrifice and death of any one of your creatures – even though the world thinks one your equal and a part of your Godhead.

We pray that you will open up our souls to the inflowing of your love, and that then will come your Holy Spirit to bring into our souls this, your Divine Love, in great abundance, until our souls are transformed into the very essence of yourself, and that there will come to us faith – such faith as will cause us to realize that we are truly your children and one with you in very substance and not in image only.

Let us have such faith as will cause us to know that you are our Father, and the bestower of every good and perfect gift, and that only we ourselves can prevent your love changing us from the mortal into the immortal.

Let us never cease to realize that your love is waiting for each and all of us, and, that when we come to you with faith and earnest aspiration, your love will never be withheld from us.

Keep us in the shadow of your love every hour and moment of our lives, and help us to overcome all temptations of the flesh, and the influence of the powers of the evil ones who so constantly surround us and endeavor to turn our thoughts away from you to the pleasures and allurements of this world.

We thank you for your love, and for the privilege of receiving it, and we know that you are our Father – our loving Heavenly Father who smiles upon us in our weakness and is always ready to help us and take us to Thy arms of love.

We pray this with all the earnestness and sincere longings of our souls, and, trusting in your love, give you all the glory and honor and love that our finite souls can give.

This is the only prayer that men need offer to the Father. It is the only one that appeals to the love of the Father, and with the answer, which will surely come, will come all the blessings that men may need, and which the Father sees are for the good of His creatures.

So, my brothers, continue to pray and have faith, and in the end will come a bestowal of the love like unto that which came to the apostles and disciples at Pentecost.

## Jesus: *"Two Kingdoms and two Choices"*
May 5th, 1917

The Kingdom of God is more peculiarly a phrase that is found in and belongs to the Christian Bible, and to some extent in the Hebrew Scriptures.

In considering the subject of this message it is first important to understand what is meant by the phrase "Kingdom of God." Some understand or conceive it to be a kingdom on earth in which the will and laws of God will be followed and obeyed by men in the mortal life, and others understand it to be that Kingdom of God which exists and will continue to exist in perfection in the spirit-world; and some few, that kingdom which will find its home or place of existence in the Celestial spheres.

Now, the way to each of these kingdoms is not the same, although in pursuing the way to one (the *Celestial Kingdom*), the way to the other must necessarily be followed. In other words, he who follows the way to the Celestial Kingdom pursues that course which in its pursuit, will cause him to do those things and obey those laws of God that are necessary to establish the kingdoms on earth and in the spirit-world. But he who pursues only the way that leads to the establishment of the kingdom on earth and in the spirit-world, cannot possibly become an inhabitant of the Celestial Kingdom.

## Jesus: *"Only one way to the Celestial kingdom"*
May 15th, 1917

As I have written before, when man was created, in addition to having bestowed upon him those things that made him the perfect man and in harmony with the laws and will of the Father, he also bestowed upon him the potentiality or privilege of receiving the Divine Love, provided he should seek for it in the only way that God had planned for its attainment. But instead of embracing this great privilege, man became disobedient and sought to exercise his own will, and did so in that manner that lead not only to his fall from the condition and the condition of the perfect manhood in which God had created him, but also to the loss of the great privilege of receiving this Divine Love, which privilege was never rebestowed upon him until my coming and teaching that rebestowal and the true way to obtain this Love.

Now, here it had better be understood what this Divine Love was and is, for it is the same today that it was when man was created in the image of God. This love differs from the natural love of man, with which he was endowed when created and which belongs to all men and which they all possess in a more or less perfect condition.

The Divine Love is that love which belongs to or is a part of God, possessing His Nature and composed of His Substance, and which when possessed by man to a sufficient degree, makes him Divine and of the Nature of God. This Great Love God intended should be received and possessed by all men who should desire to receive it and who would make the effort to obtain it.

It is the Divine Love that contains in itself the divine, which the natural love does not. Many, I know, write and believe that all men, irrespective of the kind of love they have in their souls, possess what they call "the divine spark," which needs only the proper development to make all men divine. But this conception of the state of man in his natural condition is all wrong, for man has not in him any part of the divine, and never can have, unless he receives and has developed in him, this Divine Love.

In all God's universe and creation of things material and spiritual the only one of His creatures who can possibly have within him anything of a divine nature is he who possesses this Divine Love. The bestowal of this love was intended, in its operation and effect, to transform man from the merely perfect man into the divine angel, and thus create a Kingdom of God in the Celestial Spheres, where only that which is divine can enter and find a habitation. And you must understand, that as it depends very largely upon man, himself, to establish the Kingdom of God on earth or in the spiritual world, so it also depends largely on man to establish the Kingdom in the Celestial Heavens. God will not and does not by any power that He may have establish this Divine Kingdom, and if man had never received this Divine Love into his soul, there never would have been any such kingdom brought into existence.

Then what is the way that leads to this Celestial Kingdom? The only way? For there is but one!

The way thereto is simple and single (singular) and men were taught that way by me when I was on earth; and could have been taught that way during all the centuries since I left the human life; and I must say that some have been so taught and have found that way, but comparatively few, for the mortals whose ostensible and claimed mission and privilege were to teach that way - I mean the priests and preachers and churches - have neglected to teach the same, but rather, though in earnestness and realizing their allegiance to God and their obligations to mankind, have taught merely the way which the observance of the moral precepts would lead men into.

And all this, notwithstanding, that in the Bible, which most of those professing to be Christians believe contains my sayings and teachings, is set forth this way to the Celestial Kingdom. The words are few and the way is plain, and no mystery prevents men from comprehending the meaning thereof. When I said, "Except a man be born again, he cannot enter into the Kingdom of God," I disclosed the only and true way to this kingdom.

During my time on earth there were some who understood this great truth, and since that time, there have been some who not only understood this truth, but found the way and followed it until they reached the goal and are now inhabitants of this kingdom; but the vast majority of men - priests, teachers and people - have never understood, and have never sought to find the way. This great truth to their spiritual senses has been, as it were, a hidden thing.

This Divine Love of the Father, when possessed by the soul of man, makes him in his substance and essence Divine like unto the Divinity of the Father, and only such souls constitute and inhabit the Celestial or Divine Kingdom of God.

And this being so, it must be readily seen that the only way to the Celestial Kingdom is that which leads to the obtaining of this Divine Love, which means the New Birth; and which New Birth is brought about by the flowing into the souls of men this Divine Love, whereby the very Nature and Substance of the Father, and wherefrom men cease to be the merely created beings, but become the souls of men born into the Divine reality of God.

The only way to the Celestial kingdom being by the new birth, and that birth being brought to men only by the inflowing and working of this Divine Love, and whether or not a man shall experience this birth depending in its initiative on the man himself, the question arises:

How or in what way can a man obtain this Divine Love and this new birth – and the Celestial kingdom?

The way is so easy and simple, it may be that men will doubt the truth of my explanation, and continue to believe and place all their hopes upon the doctrines of the vicarious atonement (the washing of the blood, my sufferings on the cross and bearing all the sins of the world, and my resurrection from the dead), doctrines as harmful to the salvation of mankind as they are without truth or foundation in fact or effect.

The only way then is simply this:

Man shall believe with all the sincerity of their minds and souls that this great love of the Father is waiting to be bestowed upon each and all of them, and that when they come to the Father in faith and earnest aspirations, this love will not be withheld from them. And in addition to this belief, men shall pray with all the earnestness and longings of their souls that He open up their souls to the inflowing of this love, and that then may come to them the Holy Spirit to bring this love into their souls in such abundance that their souls may be transformed into the very essence of the Father's love.

The man who will thus believe and pray will never be disappointed, and the way to the kingdom will be his as certainly as that the sun shines day by day upon the just and the unjust alike. No mediator is needed, nor are the prayers or ceremonies of priests or preachers, for God comes to man, Himself, and hears his prayers and responds thereto by sending the comforter, which is the Father's messenger for conveying into the souls of men this great Divine Love.

So, I implore men to meditate on these great truths, and in meditating believe, and when believing, pray to the Father for the inflowing into their souls of this Divine Love, and in doing so they will experience belief, faith and possession and ownership of that which can never be taken from them - no, not in all eternity. And so it is with man to choose and fix his destiny. Will that destiny be the perfect man or the Divine Angel?

**John Wesley:** *"The knowledge of these truths"*
November 15th, 1918

There is nothing in all your earth so important to mankind as the knowledge of these truths, for they deal with and affect that which belongs to the eternity of the hereafter and the future of the souls of men, and lead to a destiny which will be a divine existence.

Men are really more interested in their future destiny than in any or all things of earth and the life thereon, but give less attention to the ascertaining of the truths of the same than to many merely human things which exist only during the short earth life. They live more for the present and in a way let the future come, and find them in a condition that surprises and injures them, and makes for them a destiny that – were the truth known to them – need not be theirs.

When men shall be able to learn the truths that affect, or rather create, their destinies – if believed in and lived – they will not be so indifferent to the life of the future, even though they retain their interests in the life of earth.

And now, in this generation, when men are thinking for themselves and not resting satisfied with the dogmatic teachings of their supposed leaders, they are becoming incredulous and demanding more light, and are refusing to accept the teachings of the mysteries as satisfying to their feelings of want of those things which will give them an assurance of the truths of living as mortals.

But this does not imply – nor is it really true – that they are not in their souls interested in the eternity part of their lives and all that it means. But, becoming hopeless because they see no succor from their unsatisfied condition, they resort to the moral teachings and conduct for their salvation, having the hope that a right living in accordance therewith will result in a future as well as a present in which there must be some happiness, and that all will be well.

This, I say, is the condition of many men today, and because thereof, the ground is fallow for the planting and the nurturing of these truths.

**Matthew:** *"The salvation that Jesus taught"*
December 16th, 1918

No man or spirit can possibly receive the full salvation that Jesus taught and exemplified in his own person, who does not become wholly possessed in his soul of this Divine Love of the Father, and becomes rid of the conditions and attributes that belong to his created soul.

This soul was not created with any of the divine attributes or qualities, but simply and merely with those which you may call human and which all men and spirits who have not experienced the transformation possess.

The "God-man," as Jesus is sometimes designated by your religious writers and theologians, was not at the time of his creation (or appearance in the flesh) possessed of these divine attributes, which are of the nature and essence of the Father, but only of the human attributes which belonged to the perfect man – that is, the man who was the perfect creature as he existed before the fall of the first parents, when sin had not entered into their souls, and into the world of men's existence.

Jesus was from the time of his birth, the perfect man, and consequently without sin. All his moral qualities were in complete harmony with the will of God and the laws controlling his creation; yet, he was not greater than were the first parents prior to their act of disobedience.

There was nothing of God, in the sense of the divine that entered into his nature or constituents, and if the Divine Love had not come into and transformed his soul, he would have remained only the perfect creature of a quality no higher or greater than was bestowed upon the first man.

Jesus was as regards his possibilities and privileges, like this first man prior to his fall or death of the potentiality of becoming divine, but differed from him in this: Jesus embraced and made his own these privileges and hence became divine, while the first man refused to embrace them and lost them, and remained the mere man though not the perfect man as he was created.

And while Jesus by reason of his possession of the Divine Love became divine, yet he never became the God-man, and never can, for there does not exist and never can be a God-man. God is God alone, and never has and never can become man; and Jesus is man only, and never can become God.

Jesus is preeminently the divine man, and may rightly be called the best beloved son of the Father; for he possesses more of the Divine Love and, consequently, more of the essence and nature of the Father, than does any other spirit of the Celestial Heavens – and with this possession there comes to him greater power and glory and knowledge.

He may be described and understood as possessing and manifesting the wisdom of the Father; and we spirits of the Celestial kingdom recognize and acknowledge that superior wisdom of Jesus and are compelled by the very greatness and force of the wisdom, itself, to honor and abide in his authority.

And this transcendent and greatest possessor of the Father's wisdom is the same when he comes to you and reveals the truths of God as he is when in the highest spheres of the Celestial Kingdom clothed in all the glory of his nearness to the Father.

As the voice on the mount said "Hear ye him," I repeat to you and to all who may have the privilege and opportunity of reading or hearing his messages, hear ye him!

And when hearing, believe and seek.

**Ann Rollins:** *"Importance of knowing the way"*
March 12th, 1919

You have been told that the only way to obtain that kingdom is by the Divine Love coming into your soul and changing it into a thing divine, which partakes of the very essence of the Father Himself. Well, this is a correct explanation of the operation of this love on the soul, but in order to get this love there must be earnest supplication on the part of the seeker, and a mere mental desire for the inflowing of the love will not suffice.

This is a matter that pertains to the soul alone and the mind is not involved except, as you might say, to start the soul's longings and prayer. When you think that you are longing for this love and have a mere mental desire for its inflowing, the love will not come, because it never responds to the mere mind and must always be sought for by the soul's longings.

Many men have the intellectual desire for the love of God, and upon that desire rest, and believe that they have the love and that there is nothing further for them to do. But they will find themselves mistaken, and that instead of possessing this love they have awakened only the natural love, and in a way, started it towards its goal of the purified soul, like the first parents before the fall, and will not experience the transformation that comes with the possession of the Divine Love.

It is no easy matter to have these longings possess the soul, and men should not remain satisfied with these mere mental desires for they will not be benefited by such desires, except as I may say, in the way of having their natural love purified. The longings of the soul comes only from a realization that this love is waiting to be bestowed, and that the soul must become active and earnest in its endeavor to have this love come into it, and then the transformation takes place.

Let not your desires be only of the intellect, but try to bring into activity the longings of the soul, and do not rest satisfied until a response shall come, and it will certainly come, and you will know that the love is present working its transforming power upon the soul.

**Jesus:** *"God is the personal Father"*
April 7th, 1919

God is soul, and only soul, which has in it all the attributes of love and wisdom and thought for the welfare of His creatures. He is a thinking and seeing God, and all the energies of His soul are used to make men better and happier. As is the natural father of the man a personal father, so is the great soul of God, a personal Father to all His children; and men when they have the development of their souls in the Divine Love will know that God is personal – something more than an all enveloping energy or force or mere manifestation of His existence.

The source of things can never be the things themselves, although the things as they flow from the source have some of the qualities of the source itself, and so these manifestations of God's existence, while they are of His qualities, yet they are not equivalent of His presence or the source from which they flow. God is not everywhere, but in His Heavens, and all these expressions of His powers and will and energies are merely evidences that there is a source from which they all come, and they are not that source itself.

Every man has his own individual spirit and soul, and on the state or condition of that soul depends the happiness or misery of the man; and he is merely the brother of other men because he is a creature of God and made in His image, and not because he is a part of the universal spirit (which some people believe permeates everything and exists everywhere). God is the Father, because these children are His creatures, the objects of His creation, and individualized, each working out his own destiny. As we have told you, some of these children will always remain the merely created children, while others will partake of His Divine Love, and become a part of His divinity, and inhabitants of the Celestial spheres.

CHAPTER NINE
# FINAL RESPONSE

**Wednesday – February 4th, 2015**

**Comment**

*Dear friends and family in the Celestial realms, I come to ask your help and counsel. As you are aware, I have typed your messages and have arranged them in the form of a book that will be published with the title, "Family Reunion." In addition to the messages you have written through me, I have added a section where I provide a small selection of messages that our friend James Padgett recorded over one hundred years ago. I have the thought to now add additional messages: a response to the Padgett Messages. This, I feel, will bring this section of the book to a good end.*

*So, I ask, is there one or perhaps even several, who would desire to do this, to add a comment about the writings of James Padgett and help bring this book to a close?*

*I will now pray and then wait for your comments…*

## James Padgett: *"Where the story actually begins"*

I am here, your friend James Padgett –

I come to give a word to encourage you with this book project. It will bring influence and help to people that otherwise may not hear of the Divine Love for a very long time.

I am very pleased that you have responded to our presence and influence to bring this book to a close. I am also happy that you have responded to our suggestion to add the testimony of Helen, my beautiful soulmate, to the other testimonies that you are providing in this book. Adding the writing that Helen gave me will add a very important touch to the theme of "breaking the silence." This is where the story actually begins; for, as you know, when I began to record messages from the spirit-world, in the beginning, all that I had in my purpose was to receive messages from Helen after she passed. From this small start, the story unfolded and mushroomed into the reception of thousands of messages.

There is a comparison to be made in what you are presently doing in your work, in that you started with no foreknowledge or intention to receive messages from your own birth family now in spirit, and yet, this is what has happened. And it is a remarkable and beautiful story. It is a blessing to you and will be for those who read it.

I just wanted to come and tell you this, and to encourage you in your work, and this book.

We bless you with our love.

This is your friend, James, with Helen at my side.

## Martin Luther: *"We are always near"*

Greetings Joseph, this is Martin Luther –

There are many present, for we all have an interest in this work and the book soon to be made available to the public.

We are happy that you went first to pray before asking us to come and write; we also appreciate that you responded to our promptings about going forward with the book. It is only a beginning; we are hoping that it will be followed by another, and so we come to encourage you to continue in the work that you have begun to do. This is a team effort, and now we see it coming to pass.

I want to add that we are aware of your continuing association with friends you met at the meeting of spiritualists. This will bear much fruit. Continue to be patient; eventually you will be asked to speak to their group. This may occur in conjunction with the release of the new book, "Family Reunion."

About the book, it is good that you combined a few of the messages that James Padgett received with the messages that you recently received from us and your family. We feel what you did is very important, for it shows continuity in the messages of the Celestials to mankind.

Yes, we are aware of other responsibilities that you have that sometimes take you away from the work of receiving messages from us. Please do what you must and return, and we will be waiting to continue with our messages.

There are others present who desire to write.

We love you and appreciate the work that you do regarding the messages of truth pertaining to the Divine Love. We are always near, and we pray that you feel the presence of our love as you go about your daily life.

I love you and give you my blessings, as we know that our Heavenly Father blesses you.

I am Martin Luther, your brother and friend.


### Ana: *"Feel my excitement"*

Hello Joseph … This is Ana, your sister –

I am so happy and thrilled that you are proceeding with your book. I love the title! I am aware that you are feeling my excitement.

I just come to write a short note to join my voice with others to encourage you in this work that you are doing.

Yes, I do indeed want time with you to write messages; this will come later.

I want to say that I am happy you have thoughts about your sweet daughter, Julia Rose, to read about me and about our mother, her grandmother, Julia: all of us with the same name! This will be very interesting and important for her to read and know. We feel that she is very open to our presence and influence, though she is not yet aware of this. As you may remember, when she was young she was very much aware of us and saw us often. She will return to this sensitivity. We love her so much.

Thank you for receiving this short message. We will converse sometime in the near future.

I love you, my brother.

I am Ana – your sister.

## Thursday – February 5th, 2015

*Something that a friend wrote in a letter comes to mind. He advised me to continue to write as long as spirits come to me to give their words. I have not felt well for several days, but I feel much better today; in fact, I would love to write a message from spirit. I have pencil in hand and wait ...*

## Jesus, Luke, John and Luther: *"The greatest truth"*

Yes, Joseph, we are near and wait for you to begin…

Well, let us start then.

You have added to your book important messages that spirits wrote through James Padgett. These are good additions; for you are correct, without the Padgett Messages you would not be writing now.

How did you discover the Divine Love? Did this knowledge come as the result of your theological education while in college and seminary? What library did you visit and read about the subject of the Divine Love? Did you ever hear a preacher from a pulpit in a Christian Church declare the news about the greatest truth? And what is the greatest truth? Is it the death of Jesus on a cross and the so-called story that Jesus died for your sins?

The answer to these and similar questions is an emphatic no. You had no previous training or knowledge that the Divine Love exists, not until nine years ago when you began to read the messages received by James Padgett. There are so few books in your world that point people to the greatest truth – which is the news of the existence of the Divine Love. There is no greater truth than this.

We heard you shout, Joseph, when you were alone in your automobile and driving along the highway:

*"This is the greatest truth in all the world! Why, then, do I hesitate to tell people about it?"*

You said these words, because a person asked what kind of books you write. And your answer was feeble at best. You said: *"Spiritual books, books that have to do with the soul and our true identity."* The person that you were speaking with showed little interest, and he went on to speak of other subjects. After this, you went to your car and while driving on the highway shouted the words mentioned above. Is this accurate? Do you recall?

*Yes, of course I remember. I still feel this way today. Why do I feel so weak and hesitate to tell others about the Divine Love?*

There are things that you can do differently. But don't you see that this points to two things: Firstly, you had many experiences in the past where you were somewhat evangelical and possessed a great deal of zeal to talk to others about your Pentecostal experiences. And now, you have knowledge of the Divine Love, you hesitate to be evangelical about it.

Additionally, and this is the second point, you often doubt the degree of the Divine Love present in your soul. You have not learned yet that you are not the best judge of your own soul condition. No one on earth can accurately do this for themselves and others. You judge your experience of the

Divine Love and come to the erroneous conclusion that if you had more of the Divine Love, you would by now be changed to an extent that you would have more zeal and enthusiasm to speak to others about the Divine Love.

Do you feel that I am speaking the truth about your thoughts and opinions?

*Yes; I see myself through your words.*

Fine, Joseph; but I am here to help you see that you are mistaken about the amount of the Divine Love that is in your soul. As I mentioned above, on earth, humans have no way of knowing their own soul condition. You also seem to be forgetting something about the Divine Love: We remind you the Divine Love is waiting and available to each and every individual – but, and I say this with emphasis, BUT the Divine Love never forces its way into a soul, and no soul is ever coerced or compelled to receive it.

*I think I may know where you are heading with this ...*

Perhaps you do, and then perhaps you do not; so, allow me to continue.

We desire that you be more open about talking to people about the Divine Love. And we realize that you desire this too. Nonetheless, we do not encourage you to be more forceful about it. When asked, do not be shy or hesitant. And never demand that people listen to you. When asked, as you were the other day, do not be timid or shy about telling the truth about your books.

It is good that you had this experience as well as the outburst when you were alone in your car. You are in the process of becoming more public and the experiences you are having are an indication that you are shifting in a new direction.

People are watching and observing you. You are unaware that this is happening. Your work in public is only beginning.

Prayer for the Divine Love will never change. This is your life-line. Neglect this and feelings of weakness and unworthyness will surface again.

Now, let us return to the scene where someone asks about your books and what they are about. Consider the following. What may change the outcome is this being said:

*"The basic subject of my writings is about the greatest thing in the whole universe. The subject is God and His great love. How great is that? What a story! And I haven't really begun to tell the story the way it really is. That's why I write and continue to write."*

If something like this was said, the result might surprise you!

The truth is, Joseph, this is the kind of writing that you do, and you are not even aware that this is what you do. This subject motivates and inspires you.

Our suggestion is that you continue what you are doing, and that you not give place to the doubt of what you do and desire to do. This is the passion of your soul. There is no need to be shy about your passion. You are working to give expression to the greatest thing in the universe. How great is that! What a fantastic story!

We mentioned earlier that there really are not many writers and authors on earth producing the books that you do. As you continue doing this, there will be others who will join you; some will surpass your endeavors and this is as it should be. The more individuals – both women and men – that do this and get the word about Divine Love into the public eye, then a greater number of people will open their soul to the Divine Love and experiences of it will increase. This really is all that we desire and pray for. Now you may see more clearly why we are so interested in coming to you and give you our support, assistance and encouragement.

And so, Joseph, write and continue to write. And always be ready and willing to speak with strangers, and neighbors and friends about your work with the greatest thing in the world.

And one additional thing, when you came and sat at your desk a few minutes ago, prepared to write, you had no idea who would come to write, or what would be written. Is this not true?

*This is absolutely the truth! I was a blank slate and considered the possibility that I would not write at all.*

Good; thank you for being honest with us. Now, I ask: do you know who it is that is with you and writing this message?

*I may be wrong, but I will say it anyway. I am feeling that there are several Celestials present, namely, John the Apostle, Jesus, and of course Martin Luther.*

Well, you are nearly correct. Martin began first, then John stepped in, and then a new writer came to you – Luke, and finally, me, Jesus. Our writings merged and blended, so that you will have a difficult time identifying where one wrote and another stepped in. We are one in purpose and desire. And, in our own individual way, each of us works with you, as well as with others on earth today, to bring the message of the Divine Love to humanity.

And so, we say to you and to all other lovers of Truth: be vigilant for God's Love – vigilant and never ceasing in prayer and longing for His Great Love. Be vigilant in your writings and publishing books on the subject of the Divine Love. And be vigilant in responding to the questions brought to you by strangers.

And we say again, Love – the Divine Love – is the greatest thing in God's great and diverse universe.

We give you our blessings and encouragement. Call upon us anytime you feel the need of our presence, and we will come, for we are never but a breath away.

You are blessed by our Heavenly Father.

We are your friends and brothers …

    *Jesus*

       *Luke*

          *John, and*

             *Martin Luther.*

# GRATITUDE

I am grateful for the path called the way of Divine Love. Divine Love made the great change in my life. This is the truth I am most grateful for: the awareness of the existence of the Divine Love.

I am grateful to GOD, our Heavenly Father, Who gives the Divine Love, and makes it available to all.

I am grateful to Jesus, our beloved Master, who came to earth 2000 years ago to teach the way of Divine Love. I am grateful to Jesus, who did not give up on mankind when his message was not taught the way he presented it. I am grateful to Jesus, who found a man willing to receive his teachings to give to mankind in the twentieth century: I am grateful for James Padgett, for recording messages from Jesus, and other Celestial spirits, beginning in 1914.

I am grateful for Dr. Leslie Stone, who assisted James Padgett, and published books of the messages. I am grateful for persons responsible for placing the messages into the public domain, enabling persons like me to read the Padgett messages. And, full circle …

I am grateful to GOD, our Heavenly Father, Who showed me, through the writings of James Padgett, that the Divine Love exists, and is available to me.

I am grateful for all persons in my life who helped me toward the goal of finding the Great Love of GOD: my family – my mom and dad, all my brothers and sisters, and innumerable friends along the way of my long life. You know who you are.

Last, but not least, I am grateful to Celestial friends for their inspiration, guidance and encouragement to write this book.

To so many …

I am grateful.
*Joseph.*

FAMILY REUNION 1968
LAKE GEORGE, NEW YORK
(Bill's Summer Home)

FRONT ROW   Margie, Joe, Dorothy, Bundy, Ted
BACK ROW   Eleanor, Mother, Elmer, Marie, Ed, Bill